SHAPING
CITIES

EMERGING
MODELS
of PLANNING
PRACTICE

SHAPING CITIES

EMERGING
MODELS
of PLANNING
PRACTICE

Edited by

MOHAMMAD AL-ASAD
and
RAHUL MEHROTRA

AGA KHAN AWARD
FOR ARCHITECTURE

HATJE
CANTZ

Foreword

FARROKH DERAKHSHANI

When the Aga Khan Award for Architecture was created four decades ago, the term "architecture"—as understood by the professionals involved in shaping the built environment—did not have the same connotation in architectural discourse as it does today. The notion that architecture should improve the quality of life was not fully articulated. Planning, conservation, engineering, landscaping, slum upgrading, and innovative building technologies were considered standalone disciplines that ran parallel to architectural design rather than within it. Planning in particular plays an essential role in creating an enabling environment in which good design can flourish.

But that notion of showcasing architectural projects that were both excellent and replicable and that improved the quality of life was central to the idea that led to the creation of the Aga Khan Award for Architecture in 1977 by His Highness the Aga Khan. The very first set of awards, in 1980, juxtaposed slum-upgrading efforts, conservation schemes, engineering projects, and high tech design under the term "award for architecture," thereby expanding the definition of what architecture could be.

The desire to expand the definition of architecture has continued over the last four decades through thematic seminars and workshops that have explored issues such as housing, identity, public spaces, journalism and criticism, and workplaces.

Planning issues and their impact on our cities and other forms of settlement have always been a focus of investigation by the award. In 1982, a seminar held in Senegal entitled *Reading Contemporary African Cities* sought to analyze the rapid urbanization of a continent where many politicians and planners did not have the vision or the luxury of long-term planning. The result was huge new urban spaces presented as *faits accomplis.*

A year later, *Development and Urban Metamorphosis* was the subject of a seminar in Yemen that looked at the rapid transformation of traditional societies and the impact of change on the built environment. Another seminar, *The Expanding Metropolis: Coping with the Urban Growth of Cairo,* was held in Egypt in 1984. In this seminar the phenomenon of new metropolises such as Cairo and Mumbai was the subject of deliberation. The publication of the proceedings of these seminars in the nineteen-eighties expanded international understanding of the problems that societies faced in ever-growing urban settlements that had no guiding vision and inadequate or even nonexistent master planning.

Later, in 2012, a seminar was held in Singapore entitled *Emerging Models of Planning Practices.* The seminar was a joint project of the National University of Singapore, the Urban Redevelopment Authority of Singapore, Harvard University's Graduate School of

Design, and the Aga Khan Award for Architecture. Dean Mohsen Mostafavi and Professor Rahul Mehrotra conceived the seminar on behalf of the steering committee of the Award. This book looks back at the lessons learned and presents a selection of articles based on the papers from that seminar, as well as new contributions.

Today, planning, conservation, engineering, landscaping, slum upgrading, innovative building technologies, and cutting-edge design are integral parts of architectural discourse—in no small part thanks to efforts like those of the Aga Khan Award for Architecture. The discipline of planning, in particular, has changed dramatically. Planners now have an outsized impact on the quality of life by virtue of the scale of their vision. Today, planning is taught in universities and implemented by governments and local authorities in very different ways, reflecting its importance.

However, planning presents challenges for the Aga Khan Award. All forms of planning take a long time to implement—and the Award is confronted with the challenge of evaluating these achievements. At what stage can one see the tangible impact of the initial plans on the quality of life?

It has become evident that improving quality of life for the citizens of the world depends on the close collaboration of government agencies and planning professionals, both of which must have long-term vision and a thorough understanding of specific conditions. And it requires the creation of an enabling environment where architects, landscape architects, environmental experts, and engineers come together with private and public clients to produce better structures and public spaces, for today and for the future.

Towards New Models of
Planning Practice

MOHAMMAD AL-ASAD and RAHUL MEHROTRA

Planning today has evolved to encompass new hybrid and innovative forms of practice that are often more complex versions of earlier conventional planning approaches. Among other things, this has meant that the master plan, which we had previously understood as a definitive and encompassing instrument, has been transformed to become more inclusive, thereby recognizing its dependency on other actors and agencies for its formulation and implementation. More importantly, the validity of the master plan as a static instrument has been challenged by the fluid, quick-paced, and often unpredictable nature of contemporary urbanization. Integral to this new emerging approach are incremental strategies and multifaceted feedback loops that make the process of planning increasingly dynamic, and, in some conditions, perhaps more nuanced as well as democratic. This shift makes conventional notions of planning appear as static processes that are often without participatory protocols, and as prescriptive instruments largely focused on land use and spatial organization.

In conventional approaches to planning, advocacy, for example, which was viewed as a separate function and a form of response—and often resistance—to normative planning processes, is now viewed differently. Advocacy today has become integral to the planning process itself, and the difference between developing the tools for advocacy and engaging in advocacy has dissipated. New technologies and much freer access to data have made advocacy in the conventional (and often oppositional) sense redundant. Instead, advocacy now has become necessarily anticipatory in nature and not after the fact—something that is being increasingly acknowledged by those involved in practice as well as in the academy. The practices of planning and advocacy have become more intertwined, creating new "models of planning" that simultaneously combine both. Furthermore, with new technologies, visualization tools, and digital modes of dissemination, advocacy, implementation, and even participation have become more simultaneous. This naturally has resulted in several new formulations of what planning has come to mean, both in its practice and its pedagogy. Moreover, these nuanced forms of practice then find disparate kinds of patronage across the globe. These new, emerging forms of patronage in turn make new demands on planning, creating instant feedback loops in real time that create a condition in which planning as a practice continually morphs and evolves into new types of practices. All this challenges the singular definition of planning and its mode of practice.

In this context, "planning" as viewed through this lens of emerging "models of practice" opens up the discussion beyond narrow categories such as those of "urban planning" and/or "rural development" to include systemic ways of looking at the broader landscape in which manmade and natural habitats are situated and often comingle. In the emergent

12

contemporary context, where humanity is also virtually connected through new communication technologies, the clear physical divide between the urban and the rural is less consequential. Planning can no longer be effective in one domain, such as transportation or land use, for example, without recognizing its broader implications on other domains such as energy, affordable housing, or infrastructure.

These domains are intrinsically linked and have to be viewed and engaged in the planning imagination simultaneously. Planning as a practice therefore has become increasingly complex in its interdisciplinary engagement and dependence on the cross-fertilization of data, ideas, and action across economies, societies, and geographies. As a discipline, planning may no longer be constrained by being situated at the urban, rural, peri-urban, or regional scale. It has instead to be understood as a practice that simultaneously engages with all these terrains. It then becomes an all-encompassing field that includes urban, rural, and regional development. The reorganization of urbanizing landscapes across the globe makes it clear that inherited spatial binaries of east/west, north/south, core/periphery, and urban/rural, although useful ways to describe and organize the complex world around us, often need to be transcended since they force us to address issues through exclusive categories. In fact, planning as a discipline must, in today's world, necessarily blur binaries and not construct them. Design and planning are intrinsically about synthesis, and they involve tools that allow us to build consensus on how we as a society occupy and organize ourselves in space on this planet.

Planning accordingly also has come to include new approaches and categories such as that of "landscape and urban design," which deals with the peri-urban and regional scales, including infrastructure and its relationship to places and people. These categories encompass strategies for both brownfield and greenfield sites, and the retrofitting and renewal, as well as recycling of urban land, historic districts, suburbia, informal settlements, and new towns. In short, it features the entire gamut of conditions that are impacted by physical planning in some form. The growing attention that environmental and ecological issues have garnered in urban discourses, articulated by the considerable interest surrounding the recent emergence of landscape as a model for urbanism, are making it evident that we need to evolve more nuanced discussions for planning—discussions that overcome its traditional representation as a discipline. Furthermore, planning today is stretched even further as it attempts to grapple with issues related to the temporal and ephemeral landscapes in and outside our cities. This is further propelled by two critical phenomena. The first is the massive scale of "in-formalization" of many cities. Urban space here is constructed and configured outside the formal purview of the state. The second consists of the massive shifts in demography occurring around the globe, resulting from the search for better economic opportunities or the escape from political strife.

In this connection, a general sense of inequity that has engulfed the globe is emerging as one of the greatest challenges for planning. The operative question that comes out of this condition is: How can we imagine transitions in this unpredictable emerging landscape of demographic shifts? How can "time," a crucial component in imagining transitions, be factored into the discussion of planning? In fact, our ability to think more productively on a temporal scale in discussions of planning may play a critical role in managing this process of flux that the planet is about to experience more severely and indeed more frequently. How may planning practices respond to these newly emerging and varying conditions, and is planning as a discipline robust enough to encompass and respond to these emergent conditions?

The physical structure of human settlements around the globe is evolving, morphing, mutating, and becoming more malleable, more fluid, and more open to change than the technologies and social institutions that generate them. Urban environments today face ever-increasing flows of human movement, acceleration in the frequency of natural disasters, and iterative economic crises that modify streams of capital and their allocation as physical components of cities. As a consequence, human settlements and our relationship with nature more generally need to be imagined in different ways through more rigorous and sensitive ecological thinking. Planning of the built environment needs to be more flexible in order to be better able to accommodate nature as integral to the manmade environment. At a time in which change and the unexpected are the new norm, urban attributes like reversibility and openness seem to be critical elements for thinking about the articulation of a more sustainable form of urban development.

It is therefore becoming clearer in contemporary urbanism around the world that for cities to be sustainable, they need to resemble and facilitate active fluxes rather than static material configurations, thus shifting the emphasis from problems of space alone to those that factor in time. Ephemeral urbanism as a rubric can push us to find more complex and nuanced readings to be deployed, and new conditions to be included as part of the repertoire that surrounds discussions about planning more generally. In this context, however, the distinction between the permanent and the ephemeral is not a binary one referring to what remains versus what vanishes. It instead activates a broader concept of permanence in the sense of what is more stable, static, and persistent in relation to what is impermanent, but also of what is in a constant process of internal transformation, renewal, and reinvention, allowing for greater levels of instability. This approach embraces a longer temporal scale ranging from the effervescent forces of growth to tendencies of shrinkage, depopulation, and reabsorption—issues that have not been addressed in conventional planning practices.

Planning in its approach and in its very formulation clearly needs to be more plastic in order to be able to configure and reconfigure its operation, protocols, and processes in response to these varied conditions, and also to newly emerging forms of patronage that sometimes vary dramatically in different geographies. Planning also needs to be perceived as a series of modes of engagement or practice rather than being viewed through the usual narrow definition of planning as land use, mobility, infrastructure, and deployment of policy. There in fact are several models of practice embedded in the broader notion of "Planning Practice(s)," and these different models are relevant to different conditions. They not only engage with different physical terrains, but also embrace multiple disciplines and demonstrate probable imaginations of interdisciplinary practice and the productive crossfertilization of ideas that results from it. This approach to planning as encompassing multiple domains is critical for its future relevance. These domains simultaneously allude to and address the broader ecology that we have come to recognize in our quest to create a more sustainable planet. Planning accordingly will have to proactively embrace questions of energy, water, infrastructure, lifestyle, mobility, land use, and urban form, among others, on equal footing. It is their interconnected nature that creates a balance in the broader urban ecologies of human settlements. More importantly, it will encourage the recognition of collaborations and crossovers between otherwise seemingly disparate disciplines, thus more broadly challenging and enriching the practice and discipline of planning.

What differentiates or rather formulates these different models of practice are the varying types of patronage that they support, or by which they are facilitated. These forms of patronage bear on the political systems and ideologies that these practices serve. In today's world, they span a spectrum that ranges from the state-controlled imagination and construction of the built environment at one end, to market-led growth at the other end, with several combinations in between. The protocols and processes in each of these naturally differ, both in terms of the biases embedded in the envisioning of plans, as well as in the implementation processes that lead off from these models of practice. Needless to say, these different forms of patronage have varying political ideologies that privilege different modes and types of investments depending on particular political agendas, visions, and projections in time. These sometimes run counter to the common good of society and are influenced by different interest groups, both political and commercial. Planning has often lost its agency as a result of the neoliberal conditions that have come to prevail in many locations around the globe on account of the privatization of public services, whereas it should ideally and inherently be a matter for the state. The challenge of negotiating patronage and strategically placing its own position as a practice for the common good will perhaps be the greatest challenge for planning as a discipline in the coming decades.

Some nation states still aspire to represent their identity through the built environment and through the "city" in particular. Others have more or less given up the responsibility of projecting an "idea of the nation" through the built and physical environment as they sometimes did in their formative years by building state capitals as well as governmental and educational campuses. They have relegated this role to the private sector. In contrast, major state-directed projects today more often than not consist of highways, flyovers, airports, telecommunications networks, and electricity grids that connect urban centers, but do not contribute to determining or guiding their physical structures in a deliberate manner. This lack of explicit control over the built environment has become more complicated with the onslaught of globalization, where decisions about a given locale are often determined in another location or with non-site-specific aspirations. Here, private capital chooses to build environments that are insulated from their context, without the burdens of facilitating the sense of citizenship or place-making that is necessary in a real city. This often results in gated communities that take the form of vertical towers in the inner city, or sprawling suburban compounds at the peripheries.

State-controlled planning orchestrates the physical relationship between different classes in any society according to master plans founded upon entitlement to housing and proximity to employment. Or at least this was the aspiration and intent. In most parts of the world, the fragmentation of service and production locations in emerging economic systems has resulted in a novel, bazaar-like urbanism that has woven its presence through the entire urban landscape. This takes on multiple forms expressed in the suburban condition as well as in the landscapes of informality that are more prominent in what is referred to as the global south.

Although all this complicates planning, the challenges we face are so diverse that we need to look at multiple perspectives. As the urban scholar Eve Blau has succinctly articulated,

> *The fixed categories by which we have traditionally understood the urban and distinguished scales of design intervention have been undermined by explosive urbanization, new and unplanned patterns of migration, shifting political and economic borders, and environmental questions raised by ecological thinking ... that we need to radically recalibrate the operational lenses through which we understand and intervene in the social and physical world as urban planners, designers, and thinkers.*[1]

These massive shifts in the attitudes affecting the deployment of planning and, by extension, urban design around the world make it is useful to look at different emergent planning models at the global scale. These need not necessarily be best practices, but rather cases emblematic of the different emerging intersections between patronage, issues that are particular to a given locality, and the tools or approaches of planning employed. This book presents a sampling or series of "snapshots" of such cases and approaches from around the globe that open up questions for discussion about the future and relevance of planning as a discipline globally. Naturally, this book is not encyclopedic in its aspiration. Rather, it attempts to represent projects and approaches from practice and the academy that are grappling with the highly pluralistic emerging conditions that planning is attempting to address. The eight edited essays of this book provide a glimpse of the myriad planning approaches found in different regions across the world, including Central and South America, Europe, the Middle East, and East Asia. By covering these demographically, politically, culturally, economically, and socially diverse regions, this publication not only examines the use of conventional planning tools that concentrate on zoning, land-use policies, and transportation networks to achieve intended results, but also looks at more experimental and crossdisciplinary approaches across various geographies and societal conditions.

These essays have been written by a multiplicity of authors including officials, practitioners, academicians, and activists. Since they are often about work in which the authors have been directly involved, they therefore tend, unsurprisingly, to present that work in a positive light. Nevertheless, they do feature attempts at maintaining a level of sympathetic distance from the subject of inquiry, as is the case with Kais Samarrai's chapter on Abu Dhabi. They also feature an emphasis on the fragility of accomplishments, in spite of noted successes, as is the case in Alejandro Echeverri's chapter on Medellín. And they present particular readings as well as strong criticisms of existing conditions and directions, as is the case with Weiwen Huang's chapter on Shenzhen.

Although the chapters in this book generally emphasize specific cities or even projects in those cities, some of them explore more thematic issues that extend beyond narrowly defined geographies. Christopher Lee's chapter therefore looks into the domination of capital and market forces over the city—and the inequities that come with them—as well as how they may be mitigated through planning and design imagination. Weiwen Huang provides useful insights regarding the development of the discipline of planning in China. Bruno de Meulder and Kelly Shannon discuss how infrastructure can transcend the purely functional, and present its role in defining the quality of the urban realm. These essays accordingly resonate more globally in terms of the implications of planning as well as its instrumentality in different conditions.

The discussions of specific cities and projects on which the book concentrates address a variety of wide-ranging themes and challenges. One of the most pressing of these is the explosive population growth that has defined so many cities since the middle of the twentieth century. Abu Dhabi, Shenzhen, Cantho, Hong Kong, Singapore, and Medellín, all of which are addressed in this book, are just a few diverse examples of this phenomenon. As such cities have expanded, they have appropriated surrounding towns and rural areas; they have had to absorb overwhelming numbers of local and foreign migrants; and they have had to regularly undergo disruptive transformations regarding the structures of their urban governance and management systems. Many of the chapters in this book look, directly or indirectly, into the strategies or reactions that have come into being in order to address this massive growth of urban populations, hopefully serving as examples of a particular phenomenon as well as sources of inspiration for new formulations for the practice of planning.

Migration, both in its internal and external forms, is often the primary cause behind such explosive population growth. Internal migration in Colombia, which has been taking place since the nineteen-fifties, has heavily impacted the city of Medellín and defined the challenges it has faced. Similar conditions apply to cities throughout the emerging world. External migration has defined Abu Dhabi as well as many other affluent cities in oil-rich countries as well as industrialized and post-industrialized ones. In the case of Abu Dhabi, existing governmental regulations ensure that the migrants are temporary, but the condition of migration has become permanent, and the city's economic, social, and cultural composition is highly defined as well as challenged by the need to incorporate migrant communities, which opens up many questions regarding the limits of planning. Can such a form of temporality be planned for? Or is this inherently a condition of flux that escapes planning? Examples from the Middle East can be important when contemplating more recent conditions in Europe as it braces for the influx of distress migration from war-torn regions of the world. Can these lessons from the past inform new formulations of practice for the future agency of planning?

Another challenge defining the complex nature of today's urban development is the role of large-scale private-sector developers in the making of human settlements. The state is increasingly partnering with such investors and even relegating certain planning authorities to them. In most cases, this results in the absolution of the state's responsibility for planning. In the case of Abu Dhabi, the situation is rather ambiguous since such developers, although registered as companies, are often wholly owned by the state. The alliance between the state and the private sector is evident, for example, in the case of Shenzhen, where large-scale developers, with support from the state, are buying up and developing large properties that once consisted of "urban villages." In a city such as Hong Kong, where land values are exorbitant—therefore making it nearly impossible to limit urban densities—capital reigns supreme. More importantly, this form of planning practice further marginalizes the poor. In former, more conventional planning processes, the state would often use planning as an instrument for creating spatial and, by extension, economic equity and access. This new privatization of planning, however, is premised on the facilitation of capital accumulation that is realized through city building. Therefore, it is not human-centric by nature, and has resulted during the last decades in profound inequities that have been accelerated through spatial planning practices that have not been sensitive to the needs of the underprivileged. How then can planners be empowered to engage in these questions of inequity?

In addition to the conventional institutions of the state and private capital, other influential players, who do not neatly fit into either of these categories, are increasingly influencing the planning processes that are also effectively shaping the city. Examples of this are universities, foundations, and research complexes. These institutions often aspire to build sizable campuses, and they effectively "make" portions of the city in the process. While these newly made portions often take the form of gated communities, there have been examples where interventions are developed more sensitively and are more mindful of the context in which this form of planning is employed. This approach is explored in Dennis Pieprz's chapter through the work of his firm, Sasaki Associates, in designing the campuses of the new Singapore University of Technology and Design, and the existing Tecnológico de Monterrey in Mexico.

The conscious participation of universities as agents of urban change is already well known in a few American cities, as is the case with Columbia University in New York, the University of Pennsylvania in Philadelphia, Yale University in New Haven, and the University of Chicago. Such universities have strategically developed the historical districts in which they are located as part of an effort to transform them from the blighted neighborhoods they had become in the nineteen-sixties into highly vibrant parts of the city. The criticism has been made, however, that because of such transformations, those districts have often succumbed to gentrification and have become unaffordable to large segments of society, thus propagating conditions of inequity—particularly regarding housing, an issue from which cities throughout the world are increasingly suffering. Can planning anticipate these forms of relatively subtle displacements? Or is the agency of planning limited, depending on the regime or form of patronage it serves? Can new formulations of practice more fully encompass the broadened expectations placed on the professional planner?

In fact, the issue of inequity is another one of the many serious challenges affecting cities around the world, and the massive scale of "in-formalization" mentioned earlier is among the clearest physical manifestations of this phenomenon. Medellín provides an example of how challenges relating to inequity may be effectively addressed through spatial and planning practices. Shenzhen, by contrast, is an example of a city where current planning policies and practices have propagated inequity, marginalizing the local informal solutions that had developed in what is known as "urban villages" for providing affordable housing for rural immigrants. Christopher Lee devotes part of his chapter to addressing the issue of inequity. He presents approaches such as developing buildings with high architectural merit whose programs concentrate on public amenities that are dedicated to the service of local communities, thus collapsing architectural and planning solutions into a single entity. Planning is here instrumentalized through architectural design in anticipating the negative affects of the replacement of social housing by free-market dynamics.

This blur between urban form and planning takes on a particularly potent role when discussing the preservation or conservation of historic cities or landscapes. In Abu Dhabi, which for the most part is a twentieth century creation, there is an attempt at constructing a heritage based on notions of an Arab and Islamic past. Architecture here is instrumental in informing planning decisions, and planning focuses on preserving the architectural artifact. In the case of Hong Kong, there seems to be an acceptance of the fact that economic and financial conditions inform the preservation of heritage structures. In fact, the DNA of the city is about continuous building in increasingly high, if not absurd, densities. Older buildings, perceived as being inefficient, are being torn down and replaced by larger ones, thus erasing historical memories and associations. While soaring property prices in such a high-density environment mean that only a small number of heritage buildings may be preserved, the city's continuity with its past has come to be expressed more through its overall skyline and infrastructure networks than through its individual buildings. Planning here embraces policy and urban form to construct a new mode of engagement with the city. Here, the agency of planning becomes one that regulates the rate of change in the built environment and engages with the notion of "time" management. In fact, the instrumentality of planning is a potent one in both transforming and preserving the broader environment.

Conventional planning tools obviously continue to be used to address existing planning challenges. These are best presented in the essays about Abu Dhabi and Singapore, where top-down planning practices predominate, and at best feature limited involvement of local communities. These two examples, however, present divergent approaches within this overall direction. Abu Dhabi's oil wealth has allowed it to experiment considerably with various planning approaches and to put forward a series of planning strategies that have been implemented with varying degrees of commitment by continuously re-configured official bodies. This process of experimentation continues up to this day. Singapore, by contrast, presents a highly efficient, or rather "hyper" example of developing and implementing long-term, all-encompassing continuous planning strategies that aim at addressing the various economic, social, mobility, and environmental needs of the city and its inhabitants. Clearly, these are both cases where political systems that are able to exert tight control over the city determine its governance and its corresponding form. This of course entails the complete involvement of the state in the conventional sense of planning engagement.

We should keep in mind that all planning depends to a certain extent on the leadership, decision making, and patronage exercised by the state through its different agencies, both central and local. This of course is clearest in Abu Dhabi and Singapore, but it is also present in almost all the examples presented in the book. Even in the case of Medellín, where what has been accomplished has depended on working very closely and sensitively with the inhabitants of a number of the city's districts, such accomplishments could have only been carried out through state intervention: in implementing security measures, developing mobility solutions, or engaging in physical planning design interventions. In this case, however, it is demonstrated within the context of a democratic political climate.

Two chapters of the book present urban areas where the state is for the most part absent. One is the Kowloon Walled City in Aaron Tan's chapter on Hong Kong. Although Tan emphasizes how a local community was able to organize itself through tightly knit social and economic networks under conditions characterized by the absence of the state, it remained a district defined by overcrowding, poor sanitary levels, and criminal activity. It does not seem a place where people with a choice would want to live. It was eventually torn down. Weiwen Huang also presents in considerable detail the "urban villages" of Shenzhen, where the presence of municipal authorities is limited, but where effective, affordable informal arrangements can be provided to satisfy the housing needs of the rural poor immigrating to Shenzhen. Yet these new urban villages also suffer from problems relating to over-congestion and sanitation. They too are disappearing, as they are being sold to investors who are developing them for more affluent residents, thus displacing the rural poor who lived in them. These two examples question the range of planning by positing that the most vibrant or densest parts of the city sometimes escape the purview of conventional planning norms and attitudes. But perhaps these cases provoke us to contemplate the limits of planning—or, phrased another way: What can planning learn from these complex, accretive, extreme conditions?

Planning as a discipline and as a practice will need to work with a complex set of multidisciplinary tools in order to effectively address today's overwhelming urban challenges. From among the chapters of the book, Medellín probably provides the clearest expression. Here, such tools have even included outreach / communications initiatives that consisted of the production and dissemination of books, articles, and television programs that aimed at communicating the challenges of the city's disadvantaged districts to the rest of its residents. Also, physical interventions, whether mobility solutions, parks, or public buildings, were only carried out after extensive consultation with local inhabitants, with whom the municipal authorities engaged as equal partners. The planners addressed different domains of the city simultaneously to construct an alternate ecology that has supported urban transformation.

Unlike the essay on Medellín, the essay on Kortrijk and Cantho emphasizes tools of physical rather than economic and social intervention, but it nonetheless presents unconventional approaches within the context of traditional planning in that it shows how the urban, rural, peri-urban, and regional are brought together under the rubric of landscape urbanism. This essay presents examples of how these various scales and localities need to be addressed as an integrated whole, since they are often connected through infrastructure networks. In this context, planning and its practice place infrastructure at the center of their imaginings, positing it as the common denominator of society.

The essays in this book provide a glimpse of the tremendous complexity that faces different attempts at developing new approaches to planning our human settlements. Only relatively recently have decision makers and planning professionals begun to fully accept such complexity and to develop and adopt new planning tools as well as to recalibrate existing ones to address emergent challenges. Such complexity will only increase in the foreseeable future as cities across the globe continue to grow and expand, and as cities in post-industrialized countries continue to be reshaped according to new economic and demographic realities defined by factors such as the flight of industrial activities, the growth of migrant communities, and the increased domination of the economy by the service sector. We hope that these essays will help enrich ongoing discussions about planning in the future and, more importantly, restore to planning its speculative edge through new formulations of its practice.

1   Eve Blau, "Urbanism after Socialism," *Harvard Design Magazine: The Core of Urbanism,* 37 (2014), pp. 4–5.

ADDITIONAL READING

Rahul Mehrotra, "Negotiating the Static and Kinetic Cities: The Emergent Urbanism of Mumbai," in *Other Cities, Other Worlds: Urban Imaginaries in a Globalizing Age,* ed. Andreas Huyssen (Durham, 2008) pp. 205–18.

——, *Architecture in India since 1990* (Mumbai 2011).

Rahul Mehrotra and Vera Felipe, "Reversibility: Disassembling the Biggest Ephemeral Mega City," *ARQ* 90 (2015), pp. 14–25. Available online at http://www.scielo.cl/scielo.php?script=sci_arttext&pid=S0717-69962015000200003&lng=es&nrm=iso&tlng=en.

Power, Rights, and Emerging Forces: New Models of Urban Planning Practice in China

WEIWEN HUANG

BOOMING CITIES

In 2008, I wrote an article for *AD* magazine's *New Urban China* issue entitled "Dramatic Change and Disruptions: Urbanization in Contemporary China Observed." I mentioned in the article the amazing speed and disruptions that characterize China's urbanization process. By 2011, China's urbanization rate had hit a historic number: 50%. Thirty years ago, when China began its process of economic reform, opening its doors to the outside world, the urbanization rate was only 20%. Over 450 million rural dwellers moved to cities during this period.

The number of cities in China with a minimum of 100,000 inhabitants has increased during these past thirty years to 657. The country's urban population has increased 3.4 times, and the urban built area has dramatically risen 5.7 times. These two different rates show, among other things, a decrease in land efficiency in the newly urbanized areas. The United Nations' *2010 World Urbanization Prospects* website (http://esa.un.org/unpd/wup/) states that the number of cities in China with a population of over 500,000 inhabitants has expanded from 51 to 186 in the past thirty years. China accordingly has one-quarter of the world's cities, and also has the world's most rapid rate of urban growth. The country is expected to add approximately one hundred cities with a population of over 500,000 inhabitants during the next fifty years.

Before I entered university in 1985, I had not come across any urban planners. China today has 150,000 urban planners, as reported by the 2011 Annual National Planning Conference, a crowded and spectacular event that is organized by the Urban Planning Society of China. According to my estimates, the planning industry in China, including both national and foreign planners, employs about 300,000 people, each with a productive value of about 500,000 RMB per year (1 USD equals about 6.12 RMB). Together, they generate about 150 billion RMB (about 24.5 billion USD). Meanwhile, universities offering urban planning programs have increased from six during the nineteen-nineties to more than one hundred today.

What roles are played by the urban planning profession in China's rapid urban development? It certainly supports the country's high-speed urbanization process, and it defines the city's zoning and infrastructure frameworks. Urban planning is viewed in China as a "scientific" discipline. University programs in urban planning in China have become independent from architecture programs; urban planning has emerged as a highly sought-after field of study, and has been widely promoted as the "dragon-head of city making." The country even awarded its highest technology prize in 2011 to the noted Chinese urban planner Wu Liangyong. Moreover, there are regulations stating that no plot of land may be developed independently of an urban plan for the area in which it is located. This makes the discipline unavoidable in the urban development and construction processes.

THE ABSENCE OF RIGHTS IN PLANNING

The roots of contemporary Chinese urban planning are found in Western modernist urban planning theories and the socialist economic planning systems of the former Soviet Union, while also adhering to the needs of a centralized dictatorship. All three systems have a utopian element to them, and for the most part they subscribe to the general idea that the combination of rationalism and power can guarantee good cities with high levels of economic production and a healthy social life.

Although modernist urban planning has been criticized since the nineteen-sixties in the West, and communism largely collapsed during the nineteen-nineties, China nonetheless continues with its "Great Leap Forward" of urbanization. As China rises like a dragon, the discipline of urban planning, or the "dragon-head of city making," is growing so fast that there have been no opportunities for critical rethinking and retrospection.

The key features of the practice of urban planning in China are that it is mostly controlled by city governments; it serves an economy that promotes GDP growth and industrialization; it is a top-down, hierarchical system; it heavily promotes car-oriented cities; and although it may take into consideration criteria such as sun and shade control, and fire safety, it generally does not give much attention to the wide variety of human needs related to urban living and the human scale. All in all, it follows fixed scenarios and lacks flexibility.

Such top-down planning is heavily reliant on governmental support, and may be implemented quickly. However, since the tenure of mayors is only five years or even less, and master plans usually cover periods of ten years or longer, a number of urban planning projects often suffer from considerable discontinuity. A popular saying in China may be roughly translated as "urban planning, paper drawing, wall hanging; less work than leaders speaking!"

Planning practices in China are hierarchically organized without feedback from the grassroots level, and they often do not take the basic requirements and demands of most stakeholders into account. This is a major and systematic shortcoming.

Planning is of course a form of knowledge. In China, it is closely connected to power. Although these two elements form an integral part of contemporary urban planning in China, a very important factor—that of "rights"—is absent. Such rights include those of landowners, property owners, tenants, inhabitants, neighbors, and the general public. The subject of rights even extends to issues such as health, the environment, and cultural heritage.

The absence of rights explains many urban phenomena, such as the demolition of heritage buildings, suicides as a result of forced relocation, and farmers losing their land. The implementation of Chinese urban planning practices, with the absence of rights, is a form of violence. The mark "拆" (Demolish!), which is painted on a building's wall to announce that it is destined to be torn down, sounds like the word "China" in Chinese. It is as if the country were named "Let's demolish!"

Even though there is some self-reflection and criticism coming from within the urban planning profession, it has inevitably grown into a massive industry that faces difficulties when it comes to effective self-evaluation. The lack of market competition and user feedback, coupled with the imposition of unrealistic schedules, has meant that urban planning in China adheres to inadequate and predetermined outcomes.

INFORMAL PLANNING AS A PROTOTYPE

Is there any possibility for change? Albert Einstein once said that we cannot solve problems by using the same kind of thinking we used when we created them. We need to think outside the box and to seek inspiration and motivation from outside the conventional planning system. One example is provided by informal spontaneous constructions.

There is a ubiquity of "urban villages" in China. These are self-constructed communities composed of high-density, low-rent housing. They include traditional villages, new residences, and commercial developments that are built on collectively owned land and are surrounded by recent urban development. The social value of urban villages is not yet widely recognized. It is therefore quite common in Chinese cities such as Shenzhen—where I live—to tear them down to make way for urban renewal projects.

The Chinese system of land use follows two policies. The first is based on collective land that has not been expropriated by the government and converted into nationally held land. This land cannot be urbanized or developed. The second is land that is restored or granted by the government to villagers in exchange for expropriated land so that they may build their houses on it. This land may only be developed according to fixed parameters and for specified uses such as "residential" or "commercial." But once villagers realize the discrepancy in value between the compensation they received for expropriated land and the value of that land on the newly instituted property market, they try to make the most out of the land that remains under their ownership, and to develop it according to market prices with higher levels of density, irrespective of any policies restricting such development.

FIG. 1: Urban villages are easily recognized in the satellite images of central Shenzhen.
Their high-density morphology is an important complement to the morphology and function of
the city's formal urban planning.

Let us take Shenzhen as an example. When it became a city and a municipality was
established in 1979, Shenzhen consisted of 320 administrative villages with a total
population of about 300,000 people. The total area of buildings in those villages
occupied less than 10% (about 93 square kilometers) of Shenzhen's total built area
today. According to statistics from 2007, however, over half of Shenzhen's thirteen million
inhabitants lived in those original village buildings, thus providing for a population density
of 70,000 people per square kilometer. The other half of the population relied on housing
provided by the government (mainly for public servants) or by real estate developments
(mainly for those in the middle and upper income brackets) (FIG. 1).

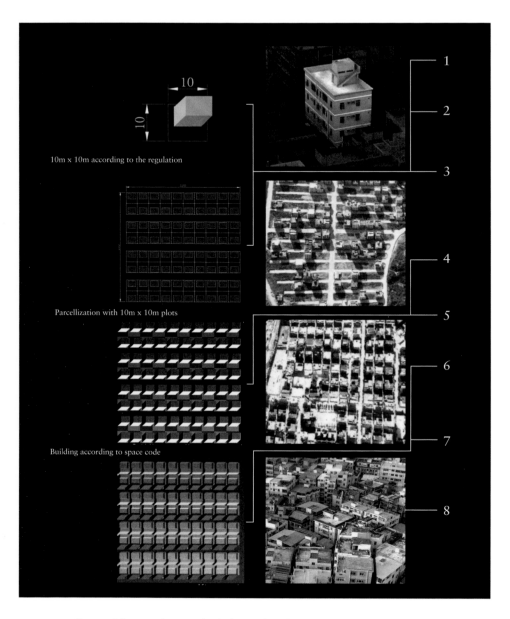

10m x 10m according to the regulation

Parcellization with 10m x 10m plots

Building according to space code

FIG. 2: Diagram showing the housing plots, housing typology, and different growth stages of Shenzhen's urban villages.

The defining characteristics of Shenzhen's urban villages were based on the household being the developer. The plot of land to be developed was 100 square meters on average. During the nineteen-eighties, typically a two- or three-story family house was built, and during the nineties, a six- to eight-story (and sometimes even higher) rental residential

FIG. 2

1
BUILDING A THEORETICAL MODEL

Why are there still so many problems
generated even after the planning
and construction of a brand new neighborhood is completed? This may be explained
through the following research model.

2
THE PLANNING STANDARD

According to the building regulation
"Planning Standards and Principles
for Shenzhen," an ex-villager's lot for a house
should not exceed 100 square meters.
The total built area should not exceed
240 square meters.

3
HOUSING TYPE

The ex-villagers generally prefer to build
single family houses with ventilation
and views (assuming a 10 x 10 meter square).
The building code requires setbacks of
8 meters from the front and back,
and 3 meters from each side. The maximum
number of houses in a 100 x 100 meter
lot accordingly should be 80 and the FAR for
4-story buildings is 1.3.

4
THE "SQUARE GRID" WAY
OF DIVIDING

The square housing type and the
setbacks specified by the building code have
determined the manner of dividing
square grid lots.

5
AMBIGUOUS AND FRAGMENTED
OUTDOOR SPACE

The "square grid" approach to dividing lots
and the square-shaped housing type created
similar lots and fragmented public spaces.

6
MARKET DEMAND FOR LOW-RENT
APARTMENTS

The city's high growth rate has
absorbed a large number of laborers from
other areas. The market for low-rent
apartments accordingly has become very
large. This drives ex-villagers to
enlarge their houses both horizontally and
vertically through additions, remodeling,
and reconstructions.

7
THE INFLATING HOUSE

The original setbacks specified by the
building code have been breached,
and the space between houses has been
reduced to less than one meter.
"Handshaking" buildings are everywhere.
Some houses are enlarged to ten
stories in height and include elevators.
The average FAR is 4.

8
THE COLLUSION OF PLANNERS
AND LANDLORDS

The formation of the "village in the city"
may be summarized as follows:

- The single square house is preferred by
  ex-villagers
- The square grid lot form is predominant
- Market-driven building expansions
  breach existing building codes
- The setbacks originally planned between
  buildings are built up
- All this has resulted in a rapid decline
  in environmental quality and in
  problematic neighborhoods

CAPTIONS: 10 x 10 meter lot size specified by the
building code, parcelization according to 10 x 10 meter plots,
building according to the building code

building with shops along the front street. The setbacks between buildings ranged from one to eight meters, creating dense concentrations of freestanding structures. Moreover, collective village stockholding corporations developed industrial and commercial facilities as well as rental properties in the collectively owned land that was mostly located next to the village's housing stock.

The high-density fabric of urban villages contrasts with the loose or massively scaled spaces of planned areas. Urban villages developed independently, and without any form of municipal oversight and regulatory procedures that would address issues such as planning, design, and building approvals, construction quality control, and property registration. Property rentals were consequently cheaper in urban villages in comparison to official developments, thus attracting low-income families, migrant workers, and low-cost businesses as well as entertainment and recreational facilities such as karaoke venues, massage parlors, and night clubs. As part of this transformation, village collective stockholding corporations that are chartered by the government took on the responsibilities of building and infrastructure maintenance, as well as providing utilities (water, gas, and electricity) and security. To a large degree, these villages operated independently of their municipalities, like autonomous enclave communities in the city (FIG. 2).

Shenzhen's urban villages essentially functioned as the city's low-income housing areas. Rents were cheap because capital outlays for construction were low, since neither the land nor any associated registration fees had to be paid. Moreover, the traditional agricultural principle of "going to work in the morning and returning at night" was the organizing principle for Shenzhen's low-income housing areas, since the villages are located next to government-sanctioned areas of the city. Every officially sanctioned commercial area, industrial park, or new center abutted a village, where workers could live cheaply and commute to work easily. In addition, the location of the villages supplemented what official urban plans had clearly

FIG. 3: The urban village of Baishizhou, Nanshan District, Shenzhen. The villagers' buildings are so close that it is possible to reach out a window and shake hands with one's neighbor. This is an image of the area's vibrant central public space, which serves as a basketball court during the day and a market at night.

FIG. 4: The night food stalls in Baishizhou's central public space.

overlooked, which was sufficient housing for low-income workers and new migrants. The existence of the villages ameliorated the effects of Shenzhen's rapid development in two ways. First, it ensured that there was enough housing to accommodate the influx of migrants. Second, the location of the villages meant that migrants lived within walking distance of their places of employment, thus lessening the need for massive investment in transportation infrastructure systems (FIG. 3).

The self-organizing development of urban villages addressed blind spots in the official urban planning process, particularly the insufficient infrastructure available for managing Shenzhen's burgeoning population. This, in turn, allowed for an improvement in efficiency and urban land functions. It also provided for a self-sufficient system of low-income housing, enriched urban services for the public, and lowered the cost of providing services and starting businesses. Shenzhen's urban villages may be viewed as a self-regulating mechanism that contributes to the efficient running of the city, and even as a type of basic urban infrastructure (FIG. 4).

Unfortunately, the important role of urban villages in Shenzhen's development was neither completely nor objectively understood. In dealing with them, planners focused instead on problems relating to high-density, sanitation, and aesthetic concerns. These issues, combined with capitalism's ongoing thirst for land to be developed and profited from, have resulted in the razing of several urban villages and their redevelopment as expensive real-estate enclaves. The owners of the villages often received satisfactory compensation through these new projects; indeed, many became wealthy as a result. Still, from the perspective of the rights of low-income segments of the population to affordable and convenient housing, and from the perspective of creating heterogeneous urban life, history, culture, space, and community, the decision to raze the villages neglected their fundamental and irreplaceable social function.

City planners and developers often overlook the important social fact that the self-organization of these villages was an urban response to the city's need for inexpensive housing. In addition, the villages contribute to the sustainability of urban networks and the heterogeneity of their social ecology. Also, as mentioned above, the convenient walking commute to the newer areas of the city releases city officials from the pressure of having to develop extensive public transportation networks. The interests of developers and the government dovetail when it comes to searching for profits and creating striking urban brands. The two therefore united to create a strong force that has razed these villages and subjected their areas to a process of urban renewal. More and more urban villages have been bulldozed. The result has been aggressive gentrification. Moreover, the pre-existing low- and middle-income housing stock, with its naturally low-carbon footprint, was gradually diminished and dismantled. As a class, migrant workers were forced to live further away from the city center. Even though the city responded by increasing invest-ment in public transportation, these new measures have not been able to substitute for the urban functions that the urban villages provided.

Urban villages are increasingly becoming the subject of evaluation and research. Plan-ning specialist John Friedmann remarked while on a fieldtrip in Shenzhen that its urban villages represent its true characteristics better than the city's planned urban spaces, which are lacking in terms of a human touch. In my 2011 article "Urban Planning and Urban Village, Who is Reforming Whom?" which I wrote for the magazine *Community Design* (vol. 45, pp. 102–06), I proposed that we learn from urban villages as an emerging urban model for the following reasons:

- Their small plot sizes make it affordable for people to own land, to build their own hous-es, and therefore to effectively participate in the making of the city.
- They support the autonomy of the community through democratic grassroots elec-tions, which are allowed and encouraged by law as a form of local governing, and also through ownership in collective stockholding corporations.
- They preserve cultural heritage and safeguard green areas following *feng shui* beliefs, and can also serve as public spaces for recreation.
- They promote pedestrian-oriented street networks.
- They incorporate a building typology that allows for mixed uses, is affordable, and cre-ates employment opportunities.
- They incorporate a process of on-site planning and design that is carried out by the local community, and are built according to the preexisting urban fabric rather than starting with a tabula rasa.

Mainstream urban planning in China, however, has unfortunately excluded the urban vil-lage prototype, even though it has much to offer. Still, those in charge of urban villages have not only been involved in constructing individual buildings, but are also becoming involved in the urban planning process. In 2006, the local village corporation of Baoan Huaide in Shenzhen decided to draft its own community planning process. Through this initiative, its residents can achieve stronger bargaining power with governmental urban planning administrators for higher densities.

AGENTS OF CHANGE

As urban villages learn from the mainstream market and mainstream planning practices, they risk losing their unique qualities and identity. This is just the tip of the iceberg in the Chinese learning process when it comes to city making. China's more economically advanced coastal cities are learning from cosmopolitan metropolises such as Singapore, Hong Kong, Las Vegas, Los Angeles, New York, and Washington, DC, China's secondary cities are in turn learning from their coastal counterparts. Eventually, the process affects small towns in the hinterland. This process has up to now been unidirectional, but I believe it should be bidirectional. Moreover, a city should learn from its own local knowledge, context, and legacy.

In China's problematic urban learning system, the emergence of third parties, which I would like to call "emerging forces," is necessary as an agent for helping people express their demands and rights as well as participate in the city making process. Fortunately, in recent years these forces are emerging powerfully in cities like Shenzhen.

These emerging forces in Shenzhen include Gongzhongli, a polling company that helps develop public opinion surveys on urban planning; City on the Bicycle, an NGO that has promoted cycling since 2006; Re-Tumu, the first NGO to be established by urban planners/architects in China, which provides design support for disaster-stricken and rural areas; Riptide, a platform that allows planners, architects, and the general public to discover unknown parts of the city; and ATU, an NGO that organizes architecture trips, lectures for architects, and activities related to architecture for children. There also is the CZC Special Force, which aims at introducing sociocratic principles (which is primarily a system of governance based on consent between people who are socially connected to each other) and is working on becoming a tenant in an urban village so as to positively intervene in the community. In addition, the Shenzhen Center for Design, which was founded in 2011, and the Shenzhen-Hong Kong Bi-city Biennale of Urbanism/Architecture, which has already completed four cycles, are both platforms that allow urban professionals to exchange ideas and rethink strategies while at the same time encouraging the participation of the general public in the planning process.

The current mechanisms defining Chinese urban planning processes essentially communicate and provide services through the existing political hierarchy and through the power of capital. It is possible, however, to reduce this imbalance between power and rights by enlisting the help of emerging, independent third parties. This tendency already exists in Shenzhen, and I believe it can become a new model for the practice of urban planning in China.

Medellín Redraws its Neighborhoods: Social Urbanism, 2004–11

ALEJANDRO ECHEVERRI

Fig. 1: View of the neighborhoods located along the slopes of Medellín's Comuna Nororiental, which has been greatly impacted by problems of segregation and violence.

THE CITY

Medellín has gone through an incredible urban and social transformation over the past fifteen years. It was considered one of the most violent cities in the world, but is now a reference regarding inclusion and social innovation processes. Any analysis of Medellín, however, should be carried out with caution, since its transformation process is in its beginnings and is defined by a social context of great inequality.

Medellín, which is Colombia's second most important city, has 3.5 million inhabitants in its metropolitan area. It is located in a valley, with the Medellín River running though its middle, and is surrounded by mountains. Its geography includes a vast number of ravines, which run down from 2,200 meters above sea level at the uppermost parts of the mountains, located along both sides of the river, to 1,400 meters at the bottom of the valley. Starting in 1950, when 350,000 people inhabited the city, it experienced explosive population growth that originated in the migration of rural populations displaced by violence. These newcomers occupied two hillsides in the northern part of the valley in which the city is located (FIG. 1).

THE REACTION TO VIOLENCE

During the nineteen-eighties and -nineties, drug trafficking came to dominate part of the city, and this made its social segregation more visible. Drug cartels dominated the younger generation of inhabitants who lived in the city's northern neighborhoods, popularly called the "Comunas." In 1991, Medellín experienced unimaginable levels of violence, and was declared the most violent city in the world, with 381 murders per 100,000 inhabitants every year, the majority of whom were young. The dramatic events of those years provoked some of the harshest and most beautiful testimonies, like Victor Gaviria's movies, *Rodrigo D: No Futuro* (Rodrigo D: No Future) and *La Vendedora de Rosas* (The Rose Seller), and the book *No Nacimos pa' Semilla* (literally, We Weren't Born for Seeds, translated as We Were not Born for Life, and Born to Die in Medellín) by Alonso Salazar. These testimonies allowed many of us to understand the real city, its spaces, its geography, its rituals and tragedies, as well as the values of its other reality. Moreover, the television program *Arriba mi Barrio* (Up with my Neighborhood), which for the first time showed and sensitized the life, territory, culture, and the inhabitants of the Comunas, became the voice of the "other" (FIG. 2).

In parallel, during the nineteen-nineties, civil society organizations, the private sector, and academia were exploring possible solutions for these conditions. Moreover, the national government created a program called Consejería para Medellín (Counsel for Medellín), which existed from 1990 until 1997 and produced the first real space for dialogue and collaborative thinking, as well as the first consensus-building processes in the city. The program supported the development of concrete actions, and these became the basis for future transformation models for the Comunas. Initiatives such as El Programa de Mejoramiento Integral de Barrios (PRIMED; Program for the Holistic Improvement of Neighborhoods), which had support from the German government, were the foundations for the strategy developed ten years later, known as Urbanismo Social (Social Urbanism).

At the end of the nineteen-nineties and during the first years of the new millennium, we began to see processes and projects that used architecture and urbanism as instruments for social change and inclusion, though not yet as holistic public policies. Instead, these were usually limited to individual efforts aimed at renovating public spaces in excluded areas of the city. The two most representative examples were the Parque de los Pies Descalzos (1999) and the Parque de los Deseos (2002). Both were promoted by Empresas Públicas de Medellín, the city's utilities provider, which is managed as a private-sector company and today generates over $500 million in revenue for the city through its investment programs. These parks highlight good design as an essential value in public projects.

FIG. 2: Cover of the 1990 book *No Nacimos pa' Semilla* by Alonso Salazar, who would be elected mayor of Medellín in 2008.

In this context, it is important to note that between 1995 and 2003, the Colombian capital Bogotá was part of an exceptional urban and cultural transformation process. Mayors Antanas Mockus and Enrique Peñalosa led three successive city governments that functioned as beacons of light in Colombian politics, particularly since this was still a time of extreme violence. They hired high-quality people to work with them. Mockus left a legacy of cultural and social programs and actions that were carried out innovatively and creatively, and that helped regain the people's trust in the city. Peñalosa's government realized unprecedented urban transformations that prioritized inclusion and the creation of public space. These excellent local administrations in Bogotá created a challenge for other cities in the country. Bogotá's example and the learning process it went through were fundamental for what was soon to take place in Medellín as well.

At about the same time, in 2002, Alvaro Uribe started his term as president of Colombia. He put forward a strategy that he named Seguridad Democrática (Democratic Security) for dealing more firmly with the guerrilla insurgency and with urban problems. Accordingly, the presence of the army and national police was strengthened in rural areas, where guerrilla groups were active, and also in cities like Medellín, where armed cartels were very strong. In 2003, the national government also signed a treaty to demobilize the pro-government paramilitary Autodefensas, which was later formalized in the Justice and Peace Law. The first handing-in of arms took place in Medellín, where initially 800 paramilitary troops handed in their weapons. Eventually, more than 4,000 such troops participated in the process and entered into a very complex process of assimilation into society. All in all, Medellín entered into a transition process that was crucial for its future evolution.

THE ACADEMY

In the nineteen-nineties, both the Universidad Nacional and the Universidad Pontificia Bolivariana (UPB) decided to focus a number of their research programs and project workshops on the neighborhoods located along the slopes of the Comunas in northern Medellín. Most of the city's social and urban problems were concentrated in this area, which was not yet sufficiently studied. It became a laboratory for social innovation and learning. Most of Medellín's informal settlements are located along its slopes, which are cut by ravines that extend from the upper part of the mountains to the river in the north. Forty percent of the city's population lives in this segregated and isolated territory, which is characterized by problems of great inequality and exclusion. The biggest challenge faced by these academic programs was the integration of these territories with the more formal city through urban projects that addressed the challenging economic and social realities mentioned above.

In 2001, I was involved with a group of professors and young professionals in creating the Taller de Proyectos del Norte (Workshop for Projects in the Northern Part of the City) at the UPB, with the purpose of developing real, concrete proposals for the neighborhoods facing problems of violence and exclusion. Through this workshop, a multidisciplinary research and consulting group began to propose a number of small-scale urban solutions as a systemic and viral strategy for transforming the urban fabric in these neighborhoods. The workshop worked directly with the communities, and focused on developing maps and documenting the everyday itineraries of the inhabitants. The resulting routes and sequences became the system for articulating programs and projects. In 2003, the then-candidate for mayor of Medellín, the mathematician Sergio Fajardo, invited us to collaborate on the development of his plan for the city. After winning the mayoral elections, Fajardo invited our team to lead the Urban Development Institute of Medellín (EDU), an established institution that works as an agency for designing and executing strategic urban projects. I was named director of EDU when Fajardo took office in January 2004. Through EDU, we led the development of the new Social Urbanism strategy, and as part of this strategy we created the concept of PUIs (Holistic Urban Projects). PUIs are an operative instrument in which the technicians in charge of physical transformations design holistic processes that simultaneously develop the conception and execution of infrastructure projects, on the one hand, and governmental programs in neighborhoods with inequity and exclusion problems on the other. It is an integrated transformation process focused on concrete, on-the-ground actions (FIG. 3).

FIG. 3: The Nor Oriental PUI (Holistic Urban Project) comprised a combination of transportation infrastructure and public spaces, as well as cultural and educational buildings.

THE POLITICS

The social forces that had arisen while the city suffered from the violence of the nine-teen-eighties and -nineties now had the opportunity to put into practice proposals that supported a more equitable city. In 1999, the civic movement Compromiso Ciudadano (Citizen's Commitment) was established under the leadership of Sergio Fajardo and the journalist and writer Alonso Salazar; they were joined by scholars, figures from the private sector, and social organizations. Compromiso is not a political party; it is a civic movement with a presence in Medellín and Antioquia, the province in which Medellín is located. It promotes and supports political candidates committed to carrying out pol-itics differently. Fajardo had run for mayor that year, but ended up in second place, as he was competing against the city's traditional political parties and power groups. He ran again, however, and won in 2003, receiving the highest number of votes that any candidate had ever received in the city's history and taking up his post as Medellín's mayor in January 2004. The high level of support enjoyed by Fajardo was a reaction to the many years of deceptive practices on the part of traditional leaders and the public's lack of trust in them.

This political development was very important in fostering the process of urban transfor-mation that Medellín is undergoing. It was then that the narrative for which Medellín has become known in recent years began. From 2004 to 2007, Fajardo led a process in which experts and leaders from diverse ideologies and backgrounds united around the shared objective of achieving structural change in the city and recovering trust in the public sec-tor through inclusive policies. Many of the actors and institutions that shared the same social sensibilities and ethical standards, and that had been searching independently for different solutions to the city's challenges, joined forces and worked closely with the public sector.

Alonso Salazar, who led the creation of the civic movement Compromiso Ciudadano to-gether with Fajardo, gave continuity to many of the programs initiated by Fajardo when he followed in his footsteps as mayor from 2008 until 2011. Salazar is the author of two books that are essential to understanding Medellín: the above-mentioned *No Nacimos pa' Semilla* (1990), which chronicles the culture of gangs in the city, and *La Parábola de Pablo* (The Parable of Pablo, 2001), which chronicles the life of Pablo Escobar, leader of Medellín's main drug cartel at the time. Salazar was a central figure in the Consejería para Medellín program as well as the director and interviewer of the testimonial television program *Arriba mi Barrio,* both mentioned above. One of the main attributes shared by Salazar, Fajardo, and other principal figures in these two periods of civic administration was the ability to build bridges and collaborative spaces for opposing actors in a city with dramatic contrasts.

The inclusion policies and programs of these two administrations were founded on a simple yet essential principle that flowed directly out of the ability of its main actors to approach and communicate with the city's reality, to give answers to citizens in excluded sectors of the city. Accordingly, this was also the essence of the various architectural and urban projects carried out by the two administrations, in which new urban spaces were conceived to foster the processes of inclusion and peaceful coexistence, and to improve the quality of everyday life in the city's neighborhoods.

Many of the processes we still see today have their origins in those crucial eight years. Medellín became a living laboratory and center for innovation through educational, cultural, and social programs that focused on its northern neighborhoods, where structural inequity and violence were most concentrated. Architecture and urbanism were the strategic tools used to make such social programs visible. Violence and crisis had caused many streets to become the territory of illegal groups. The great challenge was to make the city more transparent, to open it, to build trust, and to change perceptions of the city as a whole. A key part of this process was the transformation of public space in ways that would reestablish people's trust in their city. Social Urbanism was the strategy we used to transform and improve some of the poorest parts of the city, where we concentrated simultaneously on high-impact social programs offering new services and new, high-quality buildings, combined with new infrastructure and urban projects that connected the neighborhoods with the city's urban life. Reflecting on this urban transformation, Fajardo used to remark that "we are changing the skin of the neighborhoods of Medellín".

SOCIAL URBANISM, 2004–11

The physical transformation that has brought international attention to Medellín is the tangible expression of a profound change that is still fragile, but has had a major impact on the city's inhabitants. This transformation takes an ethical and moral position that directs its processes to respond to the excluded social contexts of the city. Designers, architects, and urban planners have been required to leave their comfort zones, and have been confronted with processes of cocreation in emerging realities of high complexity. They have had to deal with spaces of constant change that require great flexibility, but have also been offered an exceptional opportunity to assess and understand dynamic local sensitivities. Through this, they have come to deal with design as a constant learning process.

Preconceptions and stigmas present the greatest difficulties when working with historically excluded communities. For those living in such contexts, there is no distinction between "formal" and "informal" in relation to home ownership, territory, or subsistence economies. This condition is part of their daily life. It is what they know. They have developed a variety of ingenious solutions as a response to this reality. This situation demanded a quality that architects and technicians rarely have, which is the ability "to watch and listen with humility," and made them develop a more transparent understanding of local processes through dialogue and collaboration.

A major challenge facing public policies has been the need to mediate between and create spaces of contact for bottom-up dynamics and the top-down processes that characterize official programs. Developing spaces where emerging local realities and formal processes come together has required a great deal of innovation and creativity. This is where Social Urbanism, with its transformation of public space, urban itineraries, and services in individual neighborhoods, was conceived as a strategic tool. This tool included visible architecture and urban projects of various scales, government programs relating to education, culture, and inclusion, and facilitated meetings between official institutions and local organizations, as well as collaborative spaces they both could use.

Architects and other experts faced the greatest challenges when working at the borders between the consolidated and the emergent city, and in areas of the city with serious problems of scarcity and violence. The key to intervening in such informal worlds is to learn to read people's daily lives clearly. Informality requires adaptability as well as intuitive and common-sense-based processes. The tactic involved restoring dignity to the most common itineraries of daily life and using them as a chained sequence of actions and programs. Urban and architectural projects were implemented as strategic tools that created permeable processes and spatial systems. These systems, in turn, allowed for a holistic approach to the projects in question and the incorporation of more interdisciplinary work.

The experience with the urban and social transformation of Medellín over recent years has not only allowed for experimentation with the disciplines of urbanism, landscaping, and architecture, but has also been a way to create practical tools and capabilities for handling urban and social processes immersed in the dynamics of the city's politics. Although the transformation is still in its early stages, although it has to address the overwhelming challenges that Medellín faces, and although its continuity is not guaranteed—particularly in the fragile universe of Colombia's political context—these eight years (2004–11) of civic administration evolved through the efforts of Compromiso Ciudadano have offered many lessons and some clear ideas (FIG. 4).

LESSONS

- The key to success in collaborative processes between communities and government, and between technical teams and local leadership is the ability to build spaces based on respect and common language. This includes using an appropriate vocabulary shared by both parties. Moreover, trust and communication are essential to convincing different stakeholders that they can work together. All this is of course much easier said than done, because the meeting of two such different realities is fraught with misconceptions and skepticism.

- The ability to recognize values and attributes in a neighborhood's social and physical realities must be the starting point for all processes and projects. This is particularly important when working with people who deal with high levels of scarcity. We learn more from what already exists—i.e., memories, affections, codes, and local forms of construction and representation—than from anything else. We have to look for information locally and learn how to adapt it. The city is not a blank piece of paper.

44

Fig. 4: The science and technology park Explora in the New North Zone is an example
of a new public space for inclusion and meeting.

• The widespread conception of the urban project as a finite process in which infrastructural transformations are conceived as frozen moments that are developed
through a rigid, predetermined work plan, and in which the project's materiality is
separated from social dynamics, is flawed and untenable. The city's realities, especially those experienced in informally developed neighborhoods, constitute a living
process with multiple layers. It is a progressive process that cannot be defined by a
clear beginning, middle, or end, because different elements are constantly being added or subtracted. Managing this process requires an open mind and flexible spaces
of collaboration. This position redefines many concepts and principles regarding the
classical understanding of urbanism and infrastructure systems in which certainty is
a dangerous condition to assume.

• The city's transformation process must be based on the idea of addition, and on a
process consisting of multiple small-scale actions. In contrast to the conventional
way of thinking, which is based on large infrastructure systems or large-scale urban

projects, a city can be transformed and an urban system can emerge through viral progression, through the possibility of replication and multiplication that includes the repetition of small- and medium-scale projects and actions. The value of small-scale interventions should not be underestimated. Medellín's most valuable transformations between 2004 and 2011 originated in the notion of processes carried out on a local scale. This principle allows us to build many more spaces of mediation and collaboration among communities that incorporate local values. It also connects the act of design to open and dynamic processes in which multiple actors can take part.

- The sustainability of programs and projects is the result of building a process with many partners. It depends on the capacity for working with many local actors and dynamics to create projects and programs that may be adapted to different urban scales, and on the ability to use these programs and to develop a process that incorporates constant reinvention.

- The strategy of Social Urbanism relies on prioritizing certain areas of the city with social and exclusion problems. It involves designing a holistic process in order to articulate new public programs that involve different institutions and the community. The best lessons of

FIG 5: This bridge in the neighborhood Andalucía crosses the Juan Bobo ravine, which was a frontier between the armed groups that used to control the territory of Comuna Nororiental. Today, it is a meeting point on the way to a nearby Metrocable station.

Medellín come about when this process has the capacity to harmoniously bring to-gether changes to physical infrastructure with new activities, programs, and social works in neighborhoods affected by social problems and violence. They also come about when community leaders help appropriate the changes and guarantee conti-nuity and permanence, especially for programs and projects designed for that com-munity (FIG. 5).

IDEAS

Starting in 2004, important innovations were carried out in Medellín through its Social Urbanism strategy, with one the main tools being the PUIs. I worked with the municipal government until 2008. After that, I wanted to continue to explore and advance new in-novations based on what we had implemented. Based on the Medellín experience, I and a group of experts who had worked at the EDU and the people at Universidad EAFIT created URBAM, The Center for Urban and Environmental Studies at EAFIT University in Medellín in 2010.
URBAM is an agency for urban projects and a research center / think tank that is focused on emergent territories that face problems of inequity and exclusion. We see Medellín's experience as a learning laboratory. One of our objectives has been to understand and systematize the Social Urbanism strategy and the methodology of PUIs to address new challenges. Now that a number of years have passed, and as we look at what has hap-pened to some neighborhoods, we are aware of how fragile this process is—not only be-cause of political change, but also because the technical and methodological knowledge previously gained can be easily lost.
It is important to classify and define the principles we consider to be fundamental to the process. We think there are seven main ideas that have sustained the Social Urbanism strategy in Medellín. These can serve as a reference for other processes with similar characteristics, and they can open Medellin's experience to new questions and challeng-es. These seven ideas are as follows:

1. ZONES IN ACTION

It is very important to identify areas in the city with emergent processes of change that have been excluded from formal operations, and that are characterized by mar-ginal origins, a high source of conflict dynamics, and complex issues. It is very im-portant to prioritize and choose a territory with many problems and needs to be the first zone impacted in a process that is carried out in phases. In Medellín's case, the first chosen were the ones most affected by violence, the most vulnerable, and the ones that could become role models for transformation and integration with the rest of the city.

The precise definition of boundaries for areas of action operates as a framing system. It allows a detailed dissection of local needs, the recognition of the actors involved, and the identification of niche opportunity spaces. This framing system facilitates the design of a dynamic and flexible process that can be molded according to the conditions of development or intensity of urban operations. A political confluence of decisions is needed in order to develop a precise focus for the convergence of programs and projects.

Detailed knowledge and study of the zone in action is needed, as is a good relationship between the government and the communities. It is very difficult to learn about life in a neighborhood without establishing a real connection with it. In Medellín, the way to build trust and relationships is by walking the streets of the neighborhoods. Once an area is selected, trust is built through mediation and collaboration between all relevant parties. This implies the acceptance of a common language. The relationship between all parties is one of equals. Community participation produces tangible results and calls for accountability from the government.

The complexity and diversity of different interventions and participation processes, the volume and diversity of urban/architectural projects, and the new pubic programs of activities and services require that zones and projects be prioritized. These interventions require political conviction and determination. When dealing with scarce resources, political tensions often result in these resources being distributed at the convenience of the authorities, making it easy to stray from the original strategy.

2. THE CONFLUENCE OF HOLISTIC PROJECTS

PUIs have provided the most efficient instrument for designing and coordinating complex and holistic operational processes. They are holistic because physical infrastructure should not be implemented in isolation from other factors; rather, it should be conceived as part of a whole, starting with consultations regarding community interests. The resulting interventions should build social capital, citizens' trust, and communities' self-esteem.

PUIs require that all public policies be applied in one zone simultaneously and in a coordinated way, making them visible to the community. This strategy combines high-impact strategic works with local processes and small-scale interventions, and facilitates the integration of government policy programs (top-down policies) with local initiatives (bottom-up initiatives). It is a precise process that is carried out in phases with visible and verifiable objectives.

Complexity, confluence, simultaneity, and multiple scales of intervention are essential to the second idea (FIG. 6).

Fɪɢ. 6: Spain Library Park, a viewpoint park, and the Metrocable station in the Santo Domingo neighborhood. All are part of a Holistic Urban Project for Comuna Nororiental.

3. LINKING STRATEGIC PROJECTS

Zones in Action are areas that have traditionally been neglected and that have become segregated from other parts of the city. The main priority here is to break visible and invisible boundaries while linking communities with the rest of the city to transform social structures through physical projects. This will trigger tangible processes for real social inclusion.

These zones should not be viewed as separate islands. If we look at them as integral parts of the city that have temporary segregation problems, we can make an accurate reading of the expanded territory and identify opportunities for locating strategic projects and forging links. The implementation of the cable transportation system and its new stations was essential for defining this territorial strategy.

Two project types that establish such links were implemented in Medellín:
A – Projects that create new connections
B – Projects that insert new programmatic spaces

In the first category, we find new, integrated transportation systems and new urban boulevards that link "frontiers" between neighborhoods. As a result of these systems, neighborhoods that were "lost" and excluded from social and economic development are no

FIG. 7: Escalators in the Independencias neighborhood provide a form of public transportation that facilitates access to the homes along its slopes.

longer isolated. The linking of projects provides for capillary actions that connect different communities by breaking the territorial boundaries between them.

The second category is most evident in architecture and has considerable impact. The most common are parks, libraries, museums, and other cultural facilities. These buildings bring together in strategic locations a variety of cultural and educational programs as well as social services for the community.

4. TOWARDS A TRANSPARENT CITY

Recognizing the entire city in order to expand its urban, cultural, and economic dynamics has perhaps been the most valuable aspect of Social Urbanism in Medellín. Making the segregated and excluded parts of the city a visible item on the agenda of public discussions was an act of bravery that constitutes the first step towards starting a real process of inclusion. Bringing attention to previously stigmatized areas has had very positive effects on the life of the city as a whole. The transformation of Medellín became real once its citizens opened up their mental maps to include the whole city, not just fragments of it or the area where they live. This included neighborhoods whose names many had forgotten.

New works of iconic architecture with comprehensive and integral service programs are for all city inhabitants, and new, integrated transportation systems connecting these neighborhoods have been very powerful aids to building bridges as well as more functional and real mental maps of the complete city. The buildings were of the highest quality and best possible design, and served as symbols that could give an identity to many of the neighborhoods.

The new renovated itineraries, activities, and buildings have become the most effective expression of this transformation. Through these buildings, the communities of these neighborhoods are able to communicate about their conditions, thoughts, and concerns (FIG. 7).

5. QUALITY/BEAUTY: SOCIAL INCLUSION

The process of inclusion engendered by quality and beauty is largely subconscious. A strong emphasis on quality design and architecture has played a key role in creating a high sense of belonging and social recognition as well as changing perceptions of the city and its neglected communities.

Quality projects and their programs—regardless of their scale—have helped achieve a high degree of sustainability and trigger the social appropriation of public space. Elevating quality was also pursued in small interventions, as with sidewalk borders, handrails, or public staircases. All new architectural projects and urban transformations in Medellín at that time were carried out according to the highest standards. These standards were set with the participation of the relevant communities, which ensured that they felt that the projects were their own. This in turn helped reduce vandalism, for people tend to take care of what they like.

6. HEALING THE NEIGHBORHOOD'S SKIN:
PUBLIC SPACES IN WHICH TO MEET EVERY DAY

A deeper, stronger impact has been accomplished by giving people the opportunity to meet in public spaces without fear, and by creating everyday spaces for sharing and meeting, where communities can recover trust, civility, and a sense of safety. This has had a more profound impact on people's lives than any large-scale infrastructure project. An important measure of urban interaction is how much and in what ways people meet in the streets.

One of most powerful lessons we learned through Social Urbanism is to value the local. It was a process of recognizing and developing a more humble attitude when formulating projects, and of including and valuing the meaning of all that has evolved over many years of collective effort.

The tone of intervention is defined by a careful knowledge of the neighborhood's urban tissue and its local civic processes. Priority is given to developing learning processes for the technical teams that are deployed on site, which includes learning the "sounds of the street." We do not see this strategy as moral or nostalgic, so no RE-operations (renovation, reconstruction, etc.) were performed. Processes and actions were inserted in order to stitch existing ones into the city's dynamics as well as to stimulate urban healing. The tone of the operations is closer to a careful process of adding new pieces to an existing setup, rather than of total urban renewal.

It is everyday itineraries that are dignified. Streets, corners, plazas, and wherever people spend parts of their daily lives become areas for intervention (FIG. 8).

7. DESIGNING PROCESSES AND SPACES FOR MEDIATION: LEADERSHIP AND COLLABORATION

The strategic value of these new urban and architectural projects is that they are understood as ideas that frame and define zones, and that recognize local social actors and agents in order to start a process of dialogue. The process should be dynamic to allow for the identification and incorporation of new developments. It should provide for a porous and flexible space, with a well-developed ability to change and adapt. The wide range of actors, agents, institutions, and interests involved makes it almost impossible to accurately predict its conclusion, and demands a great deal of practical intelligence and common sense.

In conflict zones, it is fundamental to build spaces for mediation in partnership with local cultural groups, community leaders, and key actors. This association is required to broaden the available leadership base as well as to build a platform for trust. The process of designing projects with the communities is thus as important as the projects themselves. One of the ways to talk to communities is referred to as "talleres de imaginarios" (imagining workshops). Communities are invited to dream about a project proposal and relate it to concrete problems. Work was done with detailed plans of potential areas of intervention, and real solutions to everyday problems were identified through a collaborative process between participants and the technical teams.

Agreements and negotiations should take place directly between people, not between institutions. For each zone in action, a visible face, usually a public servant who is in charge, should be appointed as a recognizable leader and head of a high-quality team that represents an institution with clear goals and objectives. He or she should have the capacity to lead agreements and inter-institutional processes, and to generate trust among community leaders. Building trust and confidence is the key to achieving the goals set, and this may only be accomplished if the participants can agree upon a clear, straightforward agenda. Milestones may then be established to show the community that things are indeed happening and that changes are taking place.

The creation of an in-between space is what guarantees the success of the operation. Bottom-up initiatives and top-down policies need to meet on common ground.

Fig. 8: This viewpoint park in Comuna Nororiental's Santo Domingo neighborhood is one of a number of public space "balconies" in the area that overlook the city.

The recent experience of Social Urbanism in Medellín provides for many lessons, the main one being that in order to transform a reality, you need to change the common narrative in a manner that responds to a collective belief that is shared between all those involved. Another is that when the leaders of a city come up with a focused idea, they should develop it with conviction and creativity. In Medellín's case, the tipping point was the gelling of an ethical and moral position as an answer to the city's endemic problems of exclusion and violence.

But it is clear that effective processes of transformation and inclusion are still very fragile and will always be under threat for two reasons. One is political discontinuity and uncertainty. The second arises from the lack of distance that allows us to more thoroughly understand what has been accomplished in the complex and dynamic context of our city. But these threats are the subjects of another paper.

Seeding:
An Architecture of the City

CHRISTOPHER C. M. LEE

I

Urbanization used to be reactive; it was the provision of housing, amenities, and supporting infrastructure for the proletariat, a reaction to the real demands of the expanding city.[1] Today, especially in East Asia, urbanization is speculative. It is a predictive provision, based on the pressure to differentiate developments as marketable products for the developmental city—a city used primarily as a developmental tool.[2] Instigated by speculative capital and orchestrated by local governments, this form of urbanization becomes a profit-driven economic driver in itself. It places the demands of the market above all other considerations. The developmental city has a few distinct characteristics. It is often constructed from the amalgamation of speculative real estate plots, and serves up an urbanism of enclaves—fragmented and closed-off according to social class, an urban landscape of inflated and duplicated roads, spaced out towers, and oversized building blocks. The developmental city is also characterized by its tendency to define itself through its strategic positioning in opposition to other cities, often exacerbating their comparative differences to gain a competitive advantage. This tendency to overspecialize sets up distinct labor and social classes, stratifies spaces, and limits opportunities for its citizens. As the developmental city is tasked with attracting investment and human capital from the global market, the race to make and, in most instances, brand cities as unique, attractive, and livable[3] has spawned an entire list of consultants and experts: economic planners, environmental and ecological planners, infrastructure planners, city diagnosticians, transportation consultants, place-makers, resilience advisers, sustainability consultants, environment and resource management consultants, zero-energy specialists, planning process consultants, community and stakeholder engagement consultants, and urban acoustic and lighting specialists. In these circumstances, architectural and urban design, often inheriting strategies and design briefs further downstream, are consigned to the mere management of the practicalities of urbanization on the one hand, and to hubristic place promotion on the other. Coupled with a loss of confidence stemming from the failure of Modernist utopianism, they are unable and reluctant to project any alternative futures through design speculation.

Furthermore, a laissez-faire attitude towards urbanization today—to ensure the least resistance to capital taking hold in the city—results in a city that is inequitable, divided, bordered, exclusive, wasteful, and polluted, as well as economically and ecologically vulnerable. The city is dissolved, illegible to its inhabitants, and bereft of a civic dimension and a public sphere. This dissolution into a sea of enclave urbanism does not constitute the idea of the city, neither in the Western tradition as a space of plural coexistence, nor in the Chinese sense, where the city is also seen as an accommodating framework for plural coexistence, but with a clear and legible deep structure that regulates its spaces and social composition.[4]

If architecture is to make a claim for its continued relevance and simultaneously offer an alternative to the city that is now held captive to the mantras of security, comfort, and convenience, it should do so through its reification of the idea of the city as a space of equitable and plural coexistence. This is not a reenactment of the mega-Structuralists' agenda of the nineteen-sixties, which responded to the problems of the city's rapid growth with colossal architectural solutions exemplified, for instance, by Kenzo Tange's Tokyo Bay Project (1960) and Paul Rudolph's Lower Manhattan Expressway Project (1970). Neither is this connected to the misplaced faith of modernists during the nineteen-twenties in the possibility of designing entire cities based on architecture as their main component and on tabula rasa as a precondition, which is exemplified by Le Corbusier's Ville Radieuse (1924). Instead, I propose an architecture that is limited in scale, is economically and politically expedient, is familiar to its users and yet strangely different, and, most importantly, draws on its potential as a "punctuated artifact" that emanates a qualitative transformative potential, or, in other words, the seeding of an architecture of the city.

II

This notion of "seeding an architecture of the city" is an elaboration on Richard Sennett's idea of "seed planning" and a revalidation of Aldo Rossi's concept of the "urban artifact." Both these ideas rest on Aristotle's definition of the nature of the polis, or city/state. In his *Politics,* Aristotle first defines the polis as a space of association that comes into being for the sake of the common good. This space of coexistence requires both a *nomos*—i.e., constitution, law, or customs—and a physical manifestation that consecrates this space of coexistence. Considering the city as an artifact, this reification of what is common gave us the great public buildings or monuments of historical European cities, whether town houses, libraries, temples, or churches. They stand apart as "punctuators" in a consistent sea of housing, demonstrating another important embodiment of the spatial division of the polis—the public and the private realms of the city.[5]

As the city today becomes increasingly privatized, and its growth or reconstruction is driven by private capital and developed as self-contained private parcels, the continued erosion of the public realm is palpable. Thus, Sennett's recent clarion call for an open city deserves our attention. One of his strategies for making the city more inclusive, resilient, and equitable involves the practice of "seed planning."[6] This involves the strategic positing of buildings with high architectural merit that are programmed predominantly by public amenities and functions (a community center or school, for instance) in deprived areas so that communities could grow around them. He argues that this legible and finite insertion not only gives a sense of civic pride to the community, but serves as an attractor that draws well-to-do families and businesses into the area, which in time increases the diversity of the area and introduces much needed public services.[7]

What Sennett does not tell us is how to go about designing these punctuators that will instill the sense of community he speaks of. It will certainly not be the so-called "iconic architecture" so favored by private developers to differentiate their products in the marketplace. To be different and "new," these buildings twist, bend, and contort their way to media prominence. What matters here is the imageability of the container or form. The opposite is true if we are to envision an architecture that fosters a sense of belonging. Such architecture must begin with what exists—especially with what is most typical, for what is most typical is common to all.

Rossi, in his masterful reading of the historical city in *The Architecture of the City,* coined the term "urban artifacts" to describe architectures that embody the very idea of the city.[8] He argues that the urban artifact is a permanent and propelling element in the city, and that it also serves as a mnemonic structure for its citizens. Both housing and monuments can be urban artifacts if they have been involved in the continuous transforma-

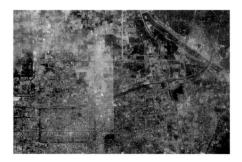

FIG. 1: Site for the proposed Horticultural Expo in the Chinese city of Xi'an.
The site is located at the northeastern corner of the city. The project brief was simply to design five greenhouses scattered around a proposed horticultural park that will anchor the expansion of the city at its northeastern corner.

tion of the city; i.e., by being a permanent element or fragment of the city and simultaneously propelling the city forward through growth and continuous use. And this continuous involvement means that the memory of the city—through use for housing and in the form of collective events for monuments—is accreted on the structures of these artifacts. Through this collective memory, the architecture of urban artifacts becomes one that is common to its citizens, an architecture of the city. Crucially, Rossi suggests that the architecture of urban artifacts is independent of function, as they have the capacity to house different programs over time, and that their irreducible structure, which comprises a specific spatial organization, has persisted through time, sanctioned by use and social acceptance.

Although *The Architecture of the City* contained no architectural proposals from Rossi, his reading of the permanent structure of the city through its urban artifacts informed the way in which he appropriated the different typologies of the historical city for his architectural projects. By abstracting the irreducible structure of urban artifacts, recasting them as fragments of the city on an architectural scale, and subjecting them to an incongruent use, his early projects—such as the Gallaratese housing project in Milan (1969–73), the San Rocco housing project in Monza (1966), and the Milan Triennale (1964)—were endowed with a quality that is rational and seemingly intuitive, familiar yet disconcertingly strange and new. As housing projects, they are intimate and grand, private and public in equal measure. This aspect of Rossi's early works is often overshadowed by his later projects, which fell into the pastiche of the historical revivals of Postmodern architecture, but they still hold many lessons on ways to architecturally articulate the idea of the seed that Sennett has sown.

III

To view an architectural punctuator as a seed is to acknowledge the temporal dimension of the project itself. This is not to say that the building will literally grow (a mistake often made by bio-mimetic designers), but that it must be flexible or "incomplete" enough to allow different uses to unfold within its framework, while maintaining its legibility and recognizability. This common artifact should draw its architectural grammar from the most typical elements of the city, and, through abstraction (and subjective interpretation), offer a new or alternative architectural proposition.

Our 2009 proposal at Serie Architects for the Xi'an Horticultural Expo design competition, which received second prize, is one attempt to draw upon the proposition outlined above. The site for this project is located at the northeastern corner of the city of Xi'an in China (FIG. 1). The brief was simply to design five greenhouses scattered around a proposed horticultural park that will anchor the expansion of the city at its northeastern corner. We felt this was inadequate in light of the vastness of the city's urban sprawl. At the same time, we were struck by the beauty and audacity of the tradition of city making in Xi'an. The city wall of Xi'an, which was built during the rule of the Tang Dynasty (618–907 AD) and measures 13.6 kilometers in length, is lodged firmly at the heart of the city (FIG. 2). It still forms an important anchoring point for the expanding metropolis despite its being breached by a sea of urbanization. As the city wall continues to reside in the collective experience and memory of the city, our proposal is an attempt to recuperate this tradition of city making by revalidating the design of the city wall.

FIG. 2: The City Wall of Xi'an. The 13.6-kilometer-long wall, which was built during the rule of the Tang Dynasty (618–907 AD), is firmly lodged at the heart of the city.

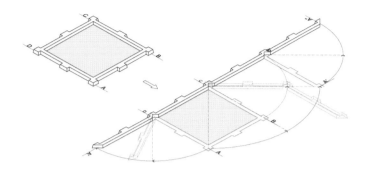

FIGS. 3 & 4: Design proposal by Serie Architects for five greenhouses for the Xi'an Horticultural Expo, 2009: Diagram of typological transformation (ABOVE); model of the proposed open linear wall. Instead of a closed quadrangle city wall (BELOW), we imagined and proposed an open linear wall that is punctuated by walled gardens and supports public amenities.

Instead of a closed quadrangle city wall, we imagined and proposed an open linear wall that is punctuated by walled gardens and supports public amenities (FIGS. 3 & 4). The wall is reimagined as a one-kilometer-long, multilevel footbridge that cuts across the horticultural park and Shibo Avenue, organizing the main circulatory path of the park and

FIG. 5: Design proposal by Serie Architects for five greenhouses for the Xi'an Horticultural Expo: Aerial perspective. The wall is reimagined as a one-kilometer-long, multilevel footbridge that cuts across the horticultural park and the Shibo Avenue motorway.

FIG. 6: Design proposal by Serie Architects for five greenhouses for the Xi'an Horticultural Expo: Interior perspective. Within the wall itself, the greenhouses are arranged as five sequential climatic zones that one may travel through.

its surrounding context (FIG. 5). Within the wall itself, the greenhouses are arranged as five sequential climate zones that one may travel through (FIG. 6). On the ground plane, pedestrian paths are woven periodically from one side of the wall to another, thereby allowing visitors to encounter various gardens on the ground level as they pass through walls in alternation (FIGS. 7 & 8). More importantly, the reinterpretation of the city wall forms a counterpoint to the city center, drawing a historical and cultural link to the city's collective imagination and creating a punctuator in a sea of urbanization. Instead of being a continuous mega-structure, our proposal presents a finite framework that functions as a common artifact, a seed that allows city life to unfold within (FIGS. 9 & 10).

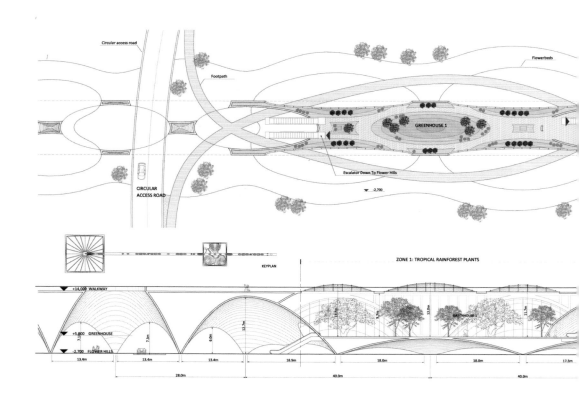

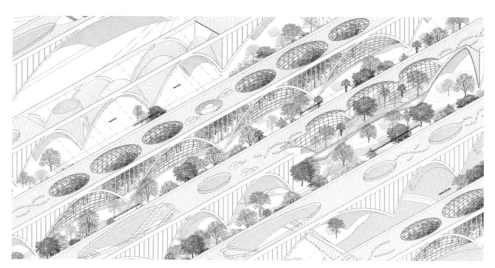

FIGS. 7 & 8: Design proposal by Serie Architects for five greenhouses for the Xi'an Horticultural Expo: Plan and elevation drawings of a section of the wall (ABOVE); collapsed isonometric of the bridge and wall (BELOW). On the ground level, pedestrian paths are woven periodically from one side of the wall to another, thereby allowing visitors to encounter various gardens as they pass through walls in alternation.

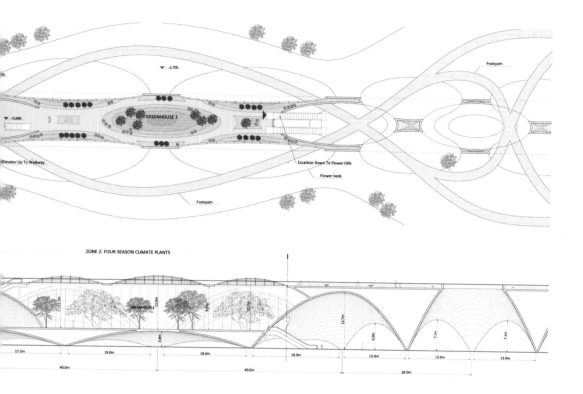

IV

Seeding an architecture of the city first requires a shift in the prioritization of the goals of urbanization. It must go beyond the mantra of security, comfort, and convenience as prerequisites for a city's competitive differentiation in the global economy. We must recognize that the city is first and foremost a space of plural coexistence, an equitable space, and a social construct, and that this very essence is challenged today by the inequity and uneven development associated with speculative urbanization. The developmental city, however, cannot be wished away that easily; any new planning practices should at least confront its excesses and aim to hold it accountable for them.

The enactment of the architecture of the city as a seed for a more diverse and plural city is not overly onerous. This may be achieved through planning tradeoffs in private developments and the use of design advisory panels in public projects to ensure high-quality architecture that engages a wide constituency and balances the demands of direct users and the general public while recognizing that the architecture of the city is at its best when it is seen as an inclusive and rarefied public art. Such architecture eschews the novel and the exotic. It alludes instead to the typical, to that which is common, sanctioned by use and cultural discourse, and tempered by time. It is punctuated, limited in its scale and extent, and forges a dialogue with the city's history and artifacts as a common work of art par excellence.

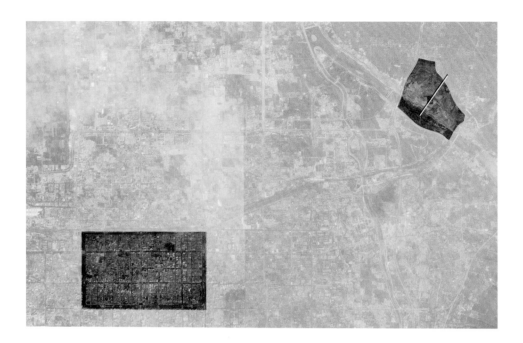

FIGS. 9 & 10: Design proposal by Serie Architects for five greenhouses for the Xi'an Horticultural Expo: Aerial collage showing the two walls of Xi'an (ABOVE); a *Capriccio* of the wall (BELOW). Instead of being a continuous super-mega-structure, our proposal presents a finite framework that functions as a common artifact and a seed that allows city life to unfold within.

1 The planned large-scale expansion of the city to meet the housing demands of workers of the Industrial Revolution in the 19th century was the genesis for the space of the urbs, the root word for urbanization. See Leonardo Benevolo, *The Origins of Modern Town Planning*, trans. Judith Landry (Cambridge, MA, 1971), pp. 105–47.

2 Manuel Castells first coined the term "The Developmental City State" to describe Singapore. For Castells, a state or city is developmental when "it establishes as its principle of legitimacy its ability to promote and sustain development, understanding by development the combination of steady high rates of economic growth and structural change in a productive system, both domestically and in its relationship to the international economy." See Manuel Castells, "Four Asian Tigers with a Dragon Head: A Comparative Analysis of the State, Economy, and Society in the Asian Pacific Rim," in *States and Development in the Asian Pacific Rim*, ed. R. Appelbaum and J. Henderson (Newbury Park, CA, 1992).

3 See Richard Florida, *The Rise of the Creative Class* (New York, 2001).

4 Christopher C. M. Lee, "The City as a Common Framework," in *Common Frameworks: Rethinking the Developmental City in China, Part 1, Xiamen: The Megaplot* (Cambridge, MA, 2013), pp. 8–26.

5 Aristotle, *Politics*, trans. Ernest Barker (Oxford, 2005).

6 This was outlined in Richard Sennett's lecture entitled "The Open City," delivered at Harvard's Graduate School of Design on September 21, 2013. Available online at https://www.youtube.com/watch?v=eEx1apBAS9A.

7 This is already evident in some areas in East London, where the insertion of well-designed schools and academies have transformed the desirability of those areas, leading to improved housing conditions and a more vibrant High Street. The dangers of gentrification that accompany such a transformation are real, but may be kept at bay when the existing stock of affordable housing is maintained by local authorities, and the provision of future stock is assured through new construction by housing associations or through planning trade-offs in private developments.

8 Aldo Rossi, *The Architecture of the City*, trans. Diane Ghirardo and Joan Ockman (Cambridge, MA, 1982).

The City Campus:
Models of Planning Processes

DENNIS PIEPRZ

Fig. 1: Monterrey, Mexico, Tecnológico de Monterrey, Sasaki Associates, 2014 (completion
of master plan); aerial view showing the university within the context of the city.
The Tecnológico de Monterrey master plan balances investment in the university campus and
the surrounding neighborhood, and builds on the conviction that a great university
requires a vibrant and successful surrounding community.

"Revolution, not evolution" was the mantra for our recent collaborative work on developing a master plan for the Tecnológico de Monterrey, the preeminent university system in
Mexico. This battle cry coming from the university's rector was neither unwarranted nor
overplayed. Monterrey, the home of the university's flagship campus, had momentarily
succumbed to growing levels of crime and vacancy due to the drug wars taking place
in parts of Mexico in recent times. An intervention by the university to restore vibrancy
and connectedness between the campus and the surrounding city could not come soon
enough. The university leaders felt a great responsibility to develop a master plan that
would both reorient the campus toward supporting a higher-order mission and develop
it into the university leader on entrepreneurship in Mexico, while also reinvigorating the
surrounding community to share in and feed long-term growth.

The success of the campus master plan and the future of the city depended on successfully integrating the city and campus. The mission and context of this project drove all aspects
of the planning, design, and implementation. A major challenge we faced, however, was
that the seventy-year-old campus, as it stood, could not support the ambitious vision to
make this flagship campus of a thirty-one-campus network the national leader in entrepreneurship education and a model of planning for the rest of Mexico (FIG. 1).

The university had an enormous task to undertake, but did manage to make the difficult leap from on paper planning to swift and impactful implementation. While there were

many factors that enabled the quick adoption and financial backing of this plan, a critical driver of what turned out to be an incredibly smooth implementation is the quality of the complex plan that is fully integrated into its social, economic, and physical contexts. This story provides for a fascinating case study to which I will return later, but let us first examine some of the universal success factors that we advocate in developing city campus plans around the world.

HOW WE WORK

What is eminently clear from working on projects like Tecnológico de Monterrey is that a rigorous process of analysis and understanding is vital to the success of urban campus planning in global contexts. Unique and diverse conditions mean that solutions cannot simply be lifted from place to place and expected to work. Context must drive planning, particularly where complex local dynamics often lead to surprising twists in the planning process. It is through deep analysis supported by technology that a true picture of what needs exist emerges to inform strategies that could feasibly fulfill them.

The first component of understanding is identifying and articulating the mission of the institution. This mission must drive the rest of the planning process. For example, a school that is moving toward collaborative cutting-edge research will require, above all, planning that supports the connectivity and cross-pollination of researchers. In contrast, a school that sees a future driven by cultivating student leadership will put far greater emphasis on generating living and learning opportunities through investment in student centers, residence halls, and cohesion between the academic core and residential life. The response to mission and context is especially critical in the planning process for a new university. Other mission mandates like achieving zero net energy by 2030 or curtailing net new building in favor of repurpose and reuse have tremendous impact on the effort and on the ways in which projects are funded and prioritized. To uncover the true mission behind a project requires engagement with diverse stakeholders combined with keen observation and expertise in the field.

Secondly, the planning team must fully understand the true dynamics of the campus before embarking on solution finding. We utilize a variety of new technologies to uncover how people connect with each other and with their surroundings, often modeling and visually mapping data to make trends intuitively graspable by all stakeholders in the community. Our approaches cluster into the following buckets:

- *Network analysis: Modeling connections, interactions, and collaborations between people.*
- *Building analysis: Analyzing the quality, condition, suitability, and operational strategies for a portfolio of buildings on site.*
- *Space analysis: Assessing how space is used and managed to maximize value.*
- *Data management: Helping clients structure and clean their data so that it can support better decision making.*

Lastly, the learned expertise and analysis of the planning team can only go so far. Once a robust understanding of the parameters of the project is uncovered so that the mission and problems at hand drive design, interdisciplinary action is the final ingredient needed to create implementable frameworks. Ideas about learning environments, place making, urban form, and mobility, as well as beauty and aesthetics all serve to create projects that inspire transformation and change.

Planning processes that incorporate the viewpoints of architects, landscape architects, economists, ecologists, investors, sustainability experts, et cetera possess a far greater likelihood of achieving successful outcomes than does an isolated planning effort. The resulting plans need to activate the public realm; integrate thoughtful programming; weave buildings with the landscape; and promote inspiring learning environments, all while keeping within the parameters established by strategic aims, budget, and capacity.

We have had the opportunity to work with premier universities around the world on change-making projects. Although each project was uniquely challenging for its own reasons, there are some similarities across projects that provide meaningful guidelines for embarking on city campus planning within a global context. The two following case studies highlight the university as a leader in sharing forward-looking visions. They also express a desire to define the twenty-first-century learning environment, a commitment to physical environments, and a hunger for deep analytical rigor.

CASE STUDY I:

Singapore University of Technology and Design (SUTD)
(the master plan was completed in 2010; construction was completed in 2015)

The SUTD master plan provided a unique challenge: to design the campus for a new university that advances the implementation of an academic vision of interdisciplinary, collaborative, and project-based learning. The university's academic mission, developed by the Massachusetts Institute of Technology (MIT) in partnership with the Singapore Ministry of Education, is based on new paradigms for integrating technology and design

FIG. 2: Singapore, Singapore University of Technology and Design (SUTD), Sasaki Associates, 2010
(completion of master plan); aerial view. SUTD is a new university that is envisioned
to be a driver of social, economic, and technological progress for the greater Singapore region.

education in the fields of Architecture and Sustainable Design (ASD), Engineering Product Development (EPD), Engineering Systems Design (ESD), and Information Systems Technology and Design (ISTD) (FIG. 2).

The SUTD is a new university that is envisioned to be a driver of social, economic, and technological progress for the greater Singapore region. Situated in East Singapore, in an area with residential and commercial uses that is located thirteen kilometers northeast of Singapore's Central Business District, the SUTD site comprises three parcels totaling twenty-two hectares. The new campus, which opened in 2015, will support a projected growth that can accommodate up to seven thousand students.

In translating this totally new pedagogical idea into a campus design, the planners and designers worked to establish a framework that would allow for a dynamic and flexible evolution of the campus.

The design connects and integrates uses through a primary pedestrian spine, an east-west "learning" corridor that reflects the university's interdisciplinary and collaborative mission. This corridor gives an address for the major program elements, and links to key adjacent uses, including the Changi Business Park, the Expo Center, and the public transit system serving the site (FIG. 3).

At the heart of the campus and the spine is the Design Center. It is the symbolic and functional hub of the university, and an international center for interdisciplinary learning and research.

Integrated around the Design Center are the academic spaces of the four academic fields (pillars) of the university. Each pillar is housed across clusters of buildings that include academic, student life, meeting, collaboration, and exhibition spaces, and each has a significant public presence on the primary spine.

Intersecting the primary academic spine at the Design Center is a north-south pedestrian corridor—or "living-learning corridor"—that connects the academic core to the

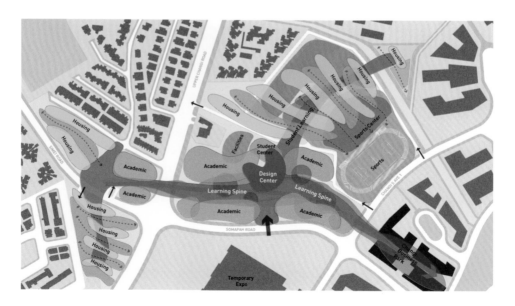

FIG. 3: SUTD, site plan with diagrams showing the relationships between the various components of the university master plan. The design connects and integrates uses through a primary pedestrian spine, an east-west corridor that reflects the university's interdisciplinary and collaborative mission, gives an address for the major program elements, and links to key community uses, including Changi Business Park, the Expo Center, and the transit system.

FIG. 4: SUTD, construction work taking place in November 2014. The master plan will be implemented through a series of architectural design competitions. The academic core complex, shown under construction in this image, was designed by UN Studio of the Netherlands and was completed in 2015

residential program. The strong connection between the academic, residential, and student life areas promotes living-learning communities and builds on the vibrancy of the campus core.

The master plan is being implemented through a series of architectural design competitions. To ensure that the aspirations of the plan are carried forward, urban design, architectural, landscape, and sustainability guidelines for building and site design are established. Singapore-based studio Surbana and Netherland-based UN Studio won design competitions for the architectural implementation, and a substantial part of the academic core and residential components were built by 2015 (FIG. 4).

Phasing of the implementation required a creative strategy to assure that each phase has a sense of place and presents an integration of uses. Phase 1 comprises the core framework and all the key components of the university, including the academic and residential spines, the Design Center, first academic clusters, residential and recreation facilities, as well as connections to a new public transit station—all these components will constitute the new university as it opens on the site in East Singapore. The academic pillars are combined within the initial academic cluster of buildings to reinforce the interdisciplinary and collaborative educational model.

The SUTD's new campus plan and academic mission reflect an aim to break new ground in interdisciplinary, collaborative, and project-based learning that can serve as a model for institutions in the region and internationally.

The master plan fosters collaboration through multifunctional academic buildings that are anchored by an International Design Center and interconnected by an outdoor pedestrian network. Like MIT's "infinite corridor," the east-west spine serves as the main pedestrian corridor of the campus, provides horizontal and vertical connections, and creates lively spaces for a wide range of university activities. Student life facilities, housing, and recreational buildings are integrated in mixed-use precincts and connected through open spaces and plazas (FIG. 5).

Sustainable design plays a large role in the campus plan, as evident in building orientation, green roofs, building systems, pedestrian and transit access, storm water

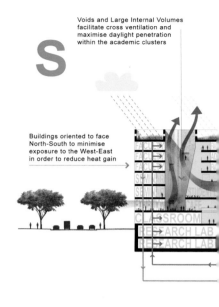

Voids and Large Internal Volumes facilitate cross ventilation and maximise daylight penetration within the academic clusters

Buildings oriented to face North-South to minimise exposure to the West-East in order to reduce heat gain

management, and in utilizing a shade canopy over the spines. The result is a campus that has a strong sense of identity, supports a vibrant community, and demonstrates the university's commitment to engaged learning and student development (FIG. 6).

The new campus is located in an area of Singapore that has developed over the past few decades, and is supported by a variety of strategic national investments. The adjacent

FIG. 5: SUTD, site plan. The master plan fosters collaboration through multifunctional academic buildings interconnected by an outdoor pedestrian network. Like MIT's "infinite corridor," the east-west spine provides horizontal and vertical connections, and creates lively spaces for a wide range of university activities. Student life facilities, housing, and recreational buildings are integrated in mixed-use precincts connected through a network of public spaces.

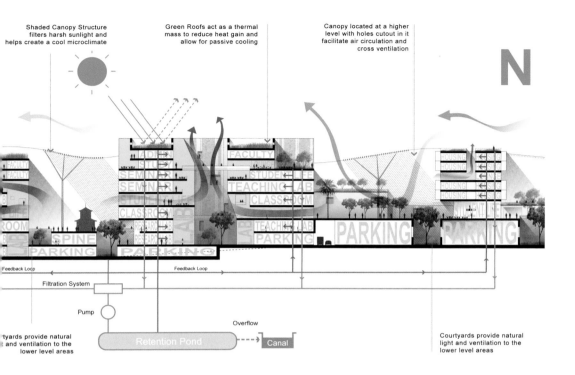

FIG. 6: SUTD, longitudinal section showing various environmentally sustainable features that are incorporated in the design of the campus. Underpinning the SUTD campus is a strong commitment to sustainability. All campus buildings face south to optimize solar orientation and minimize heating and cooling needs. To respond to Singapore's warm climate and promote climatic comfort, a canopy extends along most of the primary pedestrian spine and living-learning corridor. These architectural measures, combined with landscape strategies to promote sustainable storm water management, integrate with site-wide ecological systems and strategies.

Singapore Expo Convention and Exhibition Center and the Changi Business Park have successfully established themselves as key components of the economy. Both are served by public transit.

The business park has grown significantly since the planning of the campus began. A key idea of the university master plan is to extend the "learning spine" eastward to connect with one of the planned social cores of the business park. At the western edge, a new public transit station will directly serve the university.

Adjacent residential areas have been well established for some time. They tend to be inward focused, and therefore do not have strong physical connections to the university other than proximity. They do, however, offer a supply of faculty and staff housing with easy access to the campus.

CASE STUDY II:

Tecnológico de Monterrey, Monterrey, Mexico *(the master plan was completed in 2014; four major buildings and landscaping are to be built over the next four years)*

The Tecnológico de Monterrey (also known as the "Tec") is already the preeminent university system in Mexico, and the clear national leader in entrepreneurship. New leadership at the Tec is committed to positioning it as a catalyst for the regeneration of higher education and of the connections between universities, their communities, and the national economy. This required expanded emphasis on research, commitment to an engaged learning process, and a willingness to reconnect with the challenges surrounding the community, instead of literally fencing it off. The new president wanted "revolution, not evolution." As the flagship of a thirty-one-campus system, Monterrey could become a catalyst for nationwide integrated planning (FIG. 7).

FIG. 7: Tecnológico de Monterrey, aerial view. The design of the master plan underscores a strong commitment to strengthening the connections between the campus and the surrounding district, allowing Tecnológico de Monterrey to be a major catalyst for the transformation of the city.

FIG. 8: Tecnológico de Monterrey, diagram showing pedestrian flow patterns as produced by the MyCampus planning tool. MyCampus is a planning tool developed to allow students, faculty, and staff to participate in an online survey that mapped a series of campus conditions (such as pedestrian flow patterns) that informed the planning strategies of the framework plan.

The seventy-year-old campus, the first master-planned campus in Mexico, was tired. Recent buildings had violated the powerful sustainable integrity of the original vision. There was no culture of planning. While the campus atmosphere was vibrant and energized, it was fighting physical realities. A massive but obsolete stadium, built to house a now-departing professional soccer team and surrounded by acres of on-grade parking, occupied key land adjacent to the core. Natural academic partners were widely separated. A major classroom building actively discouraged engaged learning due to its narrow circulation and rigidly laid out conventional classrooms. In surrounding neighborhoods, a sense of danger and neglect was prevalent, and vacancy rates approached 30 percent. The purpose of the master plan was to reverse this situation, create a culture of planning, and develop an implementable vision that would immediately generate optimism and excitement.

In order to ensure effective implementation, we developed a dynamic visualization tool for prioritizing investment for more than fifty identified projects on the campus and in the surrounding neighborhood. With this tool, projects can be instantly reprioritized and placed on a timeline based on shifts in emphasis (that is, student life versus research partnerships) and available funding sources. The tool ensures that individual projects are not treated in a vacuum (FIG. 8).

An active community engagement process that the Tec initiated ensured community buy-in, as did meetings with public officials. In order to promote high-quality design, we developed conceptual designs for all high-priority projects on the grounds that simple massing does not capture the programmatic intent of a proposed building or the contribution it will make to the campus. A new library, wellness center, stadium, and the Tec Exchange meeting pavilion were all advanced through conceptual design in order to demonstrate their transformational impact on the campus and its surroundings.

The plan capitalizes on Monterrey's moderate climate to create a fully interconnected series of campus districts and to project a clear message that the whole campus is a learning environment that is committed to transparency, dialog, and engagement. In each district, whether it is the Heart of the Campus with the Student Faculty Commons complex, the cross-disciplinary learning nodes, the mixed-use R&D districts, or the park-like sweep of playing fields and sports facilities, there is a sense of connection to the larger campus and the Distrito (surrounding neighborhoods). Buildings and landscape work together to generate a powerful sense of place (FIG. 9).

The proposed Tec Exchange pavilion is a wholly new concept for a campus designed as the academic and social crossroads of the Tec, and expresses its entrepreneurial spirit. It will become a place of engagement and interaction, a building that supports action and information exchange.

In terms of lessons learned, the project illustrates the power of passion, commitment, and a wholly collaborative partnership between client and consultant. In terms of innovation, the plan takes a strong position on the importance of integrated partnerships related to applied research in a country where government research funding is limited. The plan also proposes that engaged learning, interdisciplinary collaboration, and entrepreneurial emphasis require wholly new kinds of work and learning spaces.

The project's master plan expresses a commitment to a campus that nourishes "Mind, Body, and Spirit"; to fostering a climate of collaboration and entrepreneurship; to stimulating engaged learning; to reengaging with the neighborhood and the city; and to facilitating rapid growth of research partnerships. Each is a major focus of the master plan, and each of these components of the mission is clearly addressed in an integrated fashion.

A key idea to strengthening the academic core is the creation of two "learning nodes." One emphasizes biotech and the sciences, and the other emphasizes engineering and design. Indoor and outdoor gathering spaces (with wireless Internet) are created throughout the plan to support informal learning and socializing. Academic life and social life are thought of as seamlessly integrated. Implementation of building renovations included in the master plan will comprise a physical reorganization of student services to enhance a one-stop-shopping service center already in place. Informal dining opportunities (indoor and outdoor) are included in all major projects to support student and student and faculty interaction (FIG. 10).

Our watchwords are transparency, connectivity, and collaboration, and every detail of the plan is focused on these values.

The existing campus stadium was aging and oversized, and it occupied prime land immediately adjacent to the academic core. Relocating and rightsizing the stadium enabled the creation of a major mixed-use district directly adjacent to the core campus. This would include R&D space, residential facilities for students and faculty, and playing fields that serve the campus and the larger community.

The Tec's emphasis on "Mind, Body, and Spirit" is supported by a plan to rethink student life, including a strengthening of an on-campus residential program and the creation of a centrally located comprehensive recreational center. The new district is conceived as an integrated, connected, and seamless pattern of small blocks and carefully defined public spaces with active uses such as retail and community amenities.

The new vision for the campus and district simultaneously addresses the environmental, economic, and social components of sustainable planning and design.

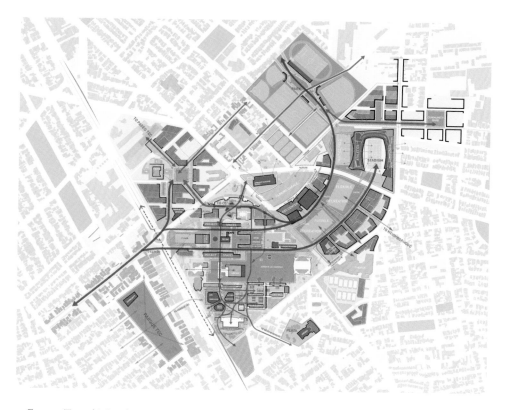

Fig. 9: Tecnológico de Monterrey, site plan showing connections between the different campus districts and the surrounding area. A new open space spine moves through Avenida del Estado, across the historical core of the original campus, connecting with the recreation fields to the north. This new district flow blurs the boundaries of the campus and ties together open space, new development, and the neighborhoods surrounding the university.

FIG. 10: Tecnológico de Monterrey, view of the Design Center. Two "learning nodes" at either end of the core campus, one emphasizing biotech and the sciences, and the other engineering and design, will create new opportunities for engaged learning across the disciplines.
They transform currently underutilized spaces into hubs of collaboration and entrepreneurship.
The Design Center encourages pedestrian connections through the complex to allow for visibility and engagement of the activities within.

The original seventy-year-old plan for the campus was highly sustainable. Buildings had optimal solar orientation; they were generally narrow in order to facilitate cross-ventilation, and they had external circulation balconies to minimize solar gain. The new master plan builds on this legacy. A comprehensive mobility and energy strategy has been

developed to enhance the performance of the campus as a twenty-first-century environment.

The plan conceives the university as a catalyst for regeneration and investment in the adjacent community and the larger urban context. Improvements in the public realm, strategic investments in the community, and the promotion of a vital economy all serve to reinforce a sustainable future for residents, students, and visitors alike. It is in large part a strategy for revitalizing the Distrito around the campus and reinvigorating the Monterrey economy.

Monterrey, long known as the safest city in Central America, suffered an increase in crime and suburban flight. With crime rates recently dropping dramatically, the city's leadership became committed to supporting closer partnerships with neighborhoods and institutions, and to investing in regeneration.

Early commitments in the planning activity include re-imagining, together with the community, the largest public park in the district. Plans for "complete streets" in many main roads in the district will improve walkability, encourage investment, ensure a higher level of security, and promote a more porous connection between the campus and the neighborhood.

The resulting plan is an inspiring and achievable vision that positions the Tecnológico de Monterrey to become the best university in Latin America, and a catalyst for regeneration and renewed investment in the neighboring districts and the greater City of Monterrey.

CONCLUSION

Universities are drivers of culture, ideas, and urban economic activity. They participate, and often lead in critical areas of social life in cities. These interactions are very much driven by local conditions and traditions. We have come to learn that when a university connects directly with its urban context, and becomes embedded in the city, both the institution and city benefit substantially. When institutions consider a long-term commitment of engagement, evolving over time to reflect the interests and needs of the community, a most effective result emerges.

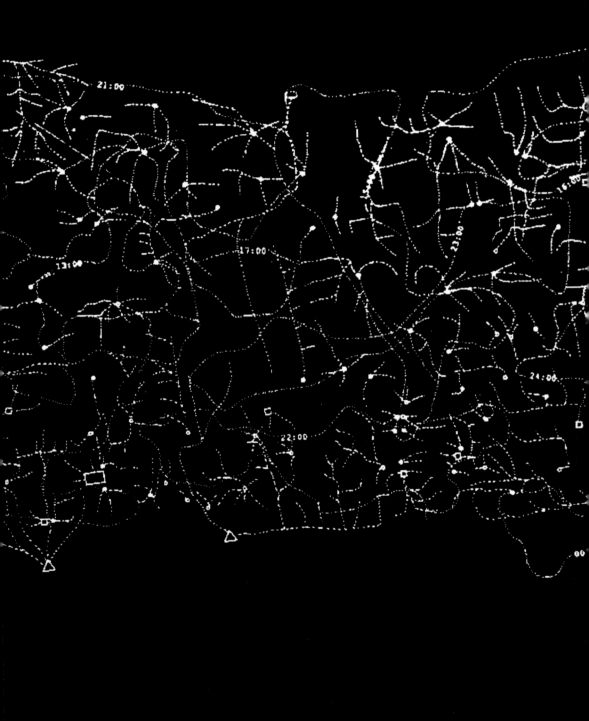

Future Heritage

AARON TAN

As my office RAD and I have been operating in Hong Kong since the mid-nineteen-nineties, I will use Hong Kong as an example to engage the questions brought up at the Aga Khan Award's seminar on emerging models of planning practices. Some of those questions are: Has economic globalization and the emergence of complex spatial developments due to new capital sources created threats to the traditional culture and urban heritage of most Asian countries? What are the roles of memories and the methods for safeguarding heritage in these developments? What are the possible sociocultural considerations in planning practices that can protect built heritage while ensuring sustainable development in contemporary Asian cities?

HONG KONG

Hong Kong is a relatively young city. Traditional, familiar nineteenth-century theories on heritage such as those of John Ruskin and Viollet-le-Duc were developed long before the reality of a city like Hong Kong could be imagined, particularly as it has emerged over the past fifty years or so. Hong Kong was founded primarily as a trade city that focused mostly on economic matters, and later especially on property development. The city has therefore experienced many rounds of building erasure and rebuilding, and not much was done to safeguard its architectural memory, at least not until the nineteen-nineties. When we compare photographs of the old and new, especially those taken from Victoria Peak, we see that almost all its old buildings have been replaced by offices and "chow laus"— literally "speculative" buildings—and ubiquitous high-rises with almost no redeeming design value that sprout like mushrooms during each economic boom. Based on these observations, it is necessary to rethink the meaning of heritage in this city, how the city can preserve memories, and what inheritances should be safeguarded (FIG. I).

EXAMPLES

Fortunately, there remain a few examples of history and memory in Hong Kong due to the more recent promotion of tourism in the city. The famous cross-harbor Star Ferry, which has operated since July 1873, and the Peak Tramway, which has operated since May 1888, are good examples, and we may refer to them as examples of infrastructural heritage.

When the Bank of China Tower by I. M. Pei and Partners was built in Hong Kong's Central District (1985–90), the existing building on its site, the mid-nineteenth-century Murray Barracks, was relocated to the city's Stanley District. The Murray Barracks building in Stanley is actually a new structure, but is clad with the original façade material. Although this may be a curious and somewhat inauthentic solution, it was a "win-win" situation. The Central District has gained a new landmark, and the Stanley District has gained a tourism icon.

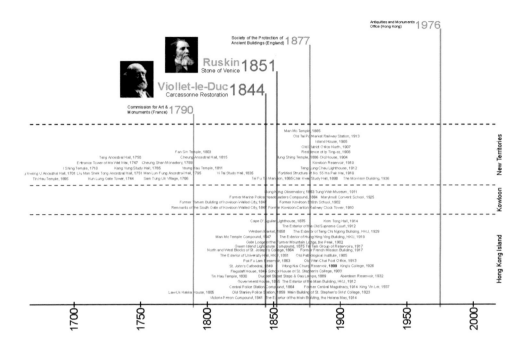

FIG. 1: A timeline showing Hong Kong's important heritage buildings from 1695 to 1937.

Inspired by this act of "reconstruction and relocation," my office and I have suggested that it would be tempting to zone a site in the New Territories of Hong Kong that would accommodate such acts of "relocated heritage" in the future. This will free more valuable land in the Central District, and will activate a remote district in the New Territories through new tourist attractions.

In another case, The Verandah Restaurant in the Repulse Bay District of Hong Kong was demolished for redevelopment during the early nineteen-eighties. Ann Hui, the movie director, wanted the Verandah for background footage, so a quick replica was built in 1984. As Hong Kong underwent a financial boom during the early nineties, the developer thought that this movie prop would add marketing value to his development. He therefore built the remaining part of the replica. The restaurant is now a very popular spot for locals and tourists, and is often used for weddings. We may label this type of accidental scenario a form of "replica preservation," in which the replica was not only preserved, but also expanded upon by the developer.

Market forces in Hong Kong continue to be the primary drive behind what stays and what goes. Because development here is highly profitable, heritage may be purchased, imported, or replicated whenever there is enough demand.

THE STAR FERRY AND QUEEN'S PIER DEMONSTRATIONS

When public demonstrations broke out in Hong Kong in 2006 to protest the demolition of the Star Ferry Pier and plans to demolish Queen's Pier, the city's authorities realized that the people of Hong Kong do in fact value heritage. The Chief Executive's office accordingly addressed issues of heritage by creating the Development Bureau in 2007. Its mandate was to protect, conserve, and revitalize the city's heritage.

This new policy shift has already helped preserve some of Hong Kong's built heritage, such as the Wo Cheong Pawn Shop in Wanchai. The developer, who won the tender to develop the adjacent site, was also required to restore the pawnshop. Both the newly restored pawnshop and the residential apartments are commercially successful. These gains came along with a priceless added benefit. Since there are no height restrictions for building in Hong Kong, new buildings reach considerable heights. In this case, since the four-story pawnshop has been preserved, the air space above it also has been preserved. As the building is located in the midst of a concrete jungle, this is a double bonus, and the result has been to safeguard both heritage and air space.

HOMEMADE HERITAGE

Local experts on conservation such as Lee Ho Yin from Hong Kong University reject demolition and reconstruction, and instead support adaptive reuse and revitalization. According to him, one cannot tell what is old and what is new in the Heritage 1881 project that the famous local tycoon Li Ka Shing built in 2009. Lee has been critical of such projects. He and other academics in Hong Kong, however, support projects that provide a contrast between a new contemporary building and an older original building on the same site, as with the 2011 Military History Museum project in Dresden by Daniel Libeskind. Interestingly enough, although Lee refers to foreign examples of designing the new to accentuate and respect the old, we also have many homemade versions of such examples throughout the city, such as the old Bank of China and the new HSBC bank buildings.

THE VALUE OF HISTORY?

The new Hong Kong heritage policy of 2007 has also classified and protected selected sites in the Central District. This has had mixed results. For example, the public, being more accustomed to appreciating the value of money rather than the value of history, has wondered why the old Police Station has been left unused for so long. It would certainly have been a different situation had the site been given to a property developer, for that would have been considered normal practice.

NEW AND UNEXPECTED CHALLENGES

The issue of dealing with heritage raises other new, and sometimes unexpected, challenges for the government. One example is the Ho Tung Garden on the Peak, which has a history of more than eighty years. The owner had a plan to replace the bungalow on the site with six villas, including one for her, but discovered that the government had classified her property as a Grade 1 heritage building. This meant that she would no longer be able to develop the project in a manner that would maximize her financial returns, which goes against Hong Kong's long-standing emphasis on the importance of property rights. Another example of such a new challenge is the Central Government Offices Complex West Wing in the Central District. A politician voted for the office to be classified as a Grade 2 instead of a Grade 1 heritage building, and accordingly was heavily criticized for not showing sympathy towards conservation.[1]

THE OLD AND NEW HSBC BUILDING

Considering the above observation, I found myself asking questions such as: Which is better, preserving what exists or building something new? Let us take Foster + Partners' 1986 HSBC building as an example. One may ask whether it would have been better to keep the old 1935 HSBC building, which already was the third HSBC building to be constructed on the same site, but which also had great heritage value. We may also ask if the right choice was made by removing it and replacing it with the new building, which may have an even greater heritage value in the future (FIG. 2).

FIG. 2: Hong Kong, views of the old 1935 HSBC building and the one from 1986
by Foster + Partners that replaced it.

FIG. 3: Hong Kong, aerial view of Kowloon Walled City from the nineteen-eighties.

A DIFFERENT PERSPECTIVE

We found it liberating to zoom out from individual examples of architecture, which in themselves are often interchangeable, and to look at the Hong Kong skyline, which is in fact of tremendous heritage value, even globally. Buildings are highly ephemeral in Hong Kong, but the skyline seems eternal. For example, once the Ritz-Carlton Hotel was built in the early nineteen-nineties, it was seriously considered for demolition, even before the first guest checked in! In fact, a new building has already been built on its site.

We therefore see that Hong Kong is not a static entity, but a living organism. One may even take the position that there is almost no need for preservation here since the city is involved in a process of self-preservation through the maintenance of its unique urban composition, which is powerfully expressed through its skyline.

KOWLOON WALLED CITY

To further elaborate on this, we may consider the now demolished Kowloon Walled City in Hong Kong (FIG. 3). It is a relevant example of the city as a living organism. It was a settlement that was capable of responding to stimuli, and also capable of reproduction, growth and development, and maintaining homeostasis as a stable whole. Kowloon Walled City, a free-for-all zone in Hong Kong, was the result of a gap that existed in Hong Kong between two political realities during the nineteen-fifties. It existed as a

Chinese-administered fortress in the British colony of Hong Kong. It may be one of the most complete examples of human/architectural symbiosis. It was almost as if its inhabitants had tapped into self-organization processes to create a particular built environment that is independent of traditional ideas of architecture. A mega-block of urban/architectural configurations, Kowloon Walled City was only about the size of four soccer fields: i.e., 200 x 150 meters, comparable in size to many of the new shopping malls in China. But it had up to 50,000 residents at its peak!

Greg Girard, with Ian Lambot the coauthor and photographer of the book *City of Darkness: Life in Kowloon Walled City* (Honolulu, 1993) took numerous photographs inside the city during the late nineteen-eighties, capturing both its exterior and interior richness. From the richness of the exterior, we are tempted to guess at the trade clusters behind the façades. The Walled City had an amazing management organization. For example, its residents and organized crime syndicates arranged for it to have its own garbage removal system. To protect a temple from being damaged as a result of litter thrown by the residents of the higher floors, a net was set up above the roof of the temple. The consequence was a beautiful shadow cast on the roof on sunny days. The city contained numerous recreation and worship spaces, particularly on the roofs. Jackie Pullinger, an evangelist who served in Kowloon from the nineteen-seventies, envisioned building a swimming pool for its drug addicts (the project was unfortunately not realized). With its people and structures in constant flux, the postman's mental map may have been the most relevant source of knowledge for this ever-changing organism.

Many have wanted to define precisely the complex relationship between humans and structures in Kowloon Walled City. This, however, was very difficult, as its physical composition was intertwined, obscured, and almost impossible to classify.

DEMOLITION

Finally, the British triumphed over the political gridlock that created Kowloon Walled City and began its demolition in the early nineteen-nineties. While this meant the death of Kowloon, it was also the only time that the dark secrets of this amazing labyrinth became available for exploration. The demolition was like slicing a loaf of bread. Every new section of the Walled City that appeared as the demolition work proceeded revealed how intricate the inhabitants' influence on the structure had been, and how quickly the structure responded to new programs. Underneath what seemed to be chaos and an absence of rules existed a sophisticated level of order and organization.

For example, the city suffered from a shortage of water and electricity. In the early days, many residents dug wells within their own properties. As later buildings were mostly ten to twelve floors in height, the residents agreed among themselves to set a schedule to pump water from these wells to the roof storage tanks. Based on the pumping schedule,

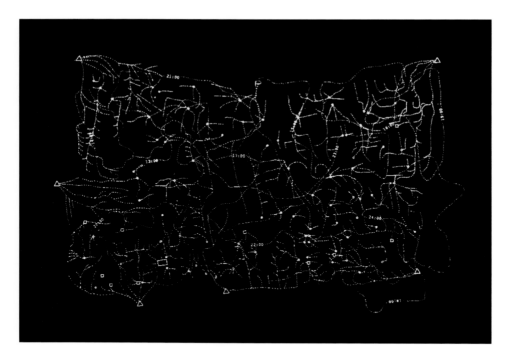

FIG. 4: Map of the water distribution network in Kowloon Walled City.

one can construct an alternative map. Such a map may help us understand the trade cluster patterns in the Walled City (FIG. 4). With so many trade clusters and food shops in Kowloon, another way to map it was based on smells.

Although the buildings were often only six inches apart, residents built extensions beyond the exterior front walls to increase their usable floor space. Through the study of the demolition, we found that the structures were modified to facilitate these extensions. There were active property developments in Kowloon with precise interpersonal contracts. Purchases of airspace and gaps often brought great financial returns. The built structures were rhizomatic in nature—interlocking, parasitic, colliding, and incoherent. Windows, doors, and stairs all had to be constantly redefined due to ongoing negotiations. While the Walled City has its unique kind of logic, it gave us the impression that the more flexible and ill defined the spatial, temporal, material, and social structures, the greater the stability of the structure as a whole.

We see the movement, interaction, and transformation between structures and human beings in Kowloon. It was an organic evolution of inorganic matter. This is an example of a symbiosis between structure and humans. It could only have taken place in Hong Kong at that time.

SEVENTEEN YEARS LATER

Seventeen years after the demolition, Greg Girard and I visited the site. We interviewed ex-residents of the neighborhood and photographed the new context. In comparing the recent photographs with those taken in the nineteen-eighties, we noticed that all sorts of activities that took place in the public spaces of the site, such as sports, gaming, and working, provided continuity with the character of Kowloon Walled City. We also collaborated on and produced an exhibition at the Hong Kong booth of the 2011 Venice Biennale entitled *Demolition as Construction*. Greg Girard stated as part of the exhibition text:

> *Seventeen years have passed and recently I went back to visit Kowloon City, the neighborhood where the Walled City once stood. With the Walled City now gone, and a park in its place, what one notices almost for the first time is how closely elements of Kowloon City resemble the Walled City. While walking the streets and alleys of Kowloon City, I was struck again and again by how many features today still resemble what I remember from the Walled City: electrical wires along hallways and external walls, the narrow staircases, the metal grillwork, the era the buildings were built, the overlap between work and recreation, and many eccentricities particular perhaps to working class Hong Kong as a whole.[2]*

HONG KONG'S URBAN DNA

Greg Girard's statement triggered the word DNA in our thinking. The people of Hong Kong may have a particular type of "urban DNA." They are by nature hard-working, have a high tolerance for crowded living conditions, and will almost do anything to earn a living. They are very adaptable and capable of transforming the built environment to meet their priorities.

RAD AS URBAN DETECTIVE

My office RAD and I explore the city as "urban detectives," looking for new urban clues and logic. We have frequently noted that at first glance, some adaptations may seem illogical, but with more analysis, we see that many adaptations are clever and have contributed to the living fabric of the city.

We were curious about the missing floor numbers in Hong Kong buildings, especially those built after the nineteen-eighties. For example, the top floor of a 34-story building on Conduit Road was numbered as the 88th floor, which implied that 54 unlucky floor numbers were omitted. As we further investigated the matter, we also found many situations where a series of buildings may have a block number 7, but a total of only six buildings. We researched several districts, from the old Kennedy town to the new West Kowloon development. We noted that many buildings have missing floors, such as 4, 13, 14, 24, ... and that some developments omitted the 40th to 49th floors. This fixation on what are considered lucky and unlucky numbers is a trend that in recent times has become more and more exaggerated (FIG. 5).

Much of this is the result of what may be referred to as tetraphobia: the fear of the "unlucky" number four. The number "4" sounds similar to the word "death" in Cantonese. As this new system is only related to existing "lucky" and "unlucky" numbers, we have wondered if maximizing the "lucky" floor numbers that a building can possess is the next logical step. Will there soon be buildings with floors numbered only with the numbers 2, 3, 5, 6, 7, 8, 9 ... (i.e., numbers that are not considered "bad")? Rather than seeing this trend merely the result of superstition, we wonder if we can turn it into an urban opportunity (FIG. 6).

Although unlucky numbers such as 4 and 44 are slowly disappearing from our urban numerical ecosystem, would it be possible to resurrect these numbers and

FIG. 5: Shanghai, an elevator button panel in a residential apartment building with floor numbers 4, 13, and 14 omitted.

FIG. 6: A list of numbers that are considered lucky and unlucky in Chinese culture. Unlucky numbers are an expression of "tetraphobia," which is the practice of avoiding instances of the number 4 in Chinese culture.

create a new urban catalyst at the same time? With these questions, we made a proposal at the 2010 Hong Kong–Shenzhen Biennale. In the biennale exhibition *Discovering Possibilities; Revealing Potential*, we reintroduced the missing floors into the buildings that once deleted these "unlucky" floors. We proposed new programs for the public, from education to recreation. We also recommended that the public should propose how to use these spaces. These spaces may be further connected through link bridges, which are commonly used in Hong Kong (FIGS. 7, 8, 9, & 10).

FIG. 7: An edited photograph of two buildings in Hong Kong's West Kowloon district showing horizontal gaps inserted where the unnumbered unlucky floors would have existed.

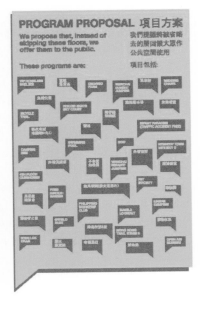

FIGS. 8, 9, & 10: Models for an exhibition that RAD developed for the 2010
Hong Kong–Shenzhen Biennale in which we reintroduced the missing floors into the buildings that
once deleted what are considered unlucky floors. To fill them in, we also proposed new
programs for the public that range from education to recreation. We also recommended that the
public should propose how to use these spaces. These spaces may be further connected
through bridges, which are commonly used in Hong Kong.

We believe that the people of Hong Kong—who have made Kowloon Walled City, who
have transformed the public space under Foster's HSBC building into an area that is
actively used by local and foreign domestic helpers during the weekends, and who
have introduced escalators connecting the business district to expensive residences
in order to help their residents avoid having to drive through areas of heavy vehicular
traffic—will know best how to reclaim these missing floors. Kowloon Walled City was
made in the most ambiguous and difficult of situations, and the same resilient Hong
Kong urban DNA will know how to transform these new roofs, how to link these missing

FIG. 11: RAD's poster for its exhibition *Discovering Possibilities; Revealing Potential*
at the 2010 Hong Kong–Shenzhen Biennale.

floors, how to engage the ground, and how to eventually make an interesting impact at
the scale of the city. The exhibition we featured at the Hong Kong–Shenzhen Biennale
aimed at exploring how tetraphobia may lead to several new possibilities and potentials
for the city (FIG. 11).

I do not have a definite conclusion with respect to the questions raised at the Aga Khan
Award for Architecture seminar, as my office and I are operating in a unique and inde-
terminate city set in constant flux. Perhaps beyond the traditional theories of Ruskin
or Viollet-le-Duc, we see ourselves more as twenty-first-century explorers, looking for
clues and catalysts that help the living organism of Hong Kong continue its self-preservation. We are moving from preserving architecture to preserving ideas.

1 The grades that the Antiquities Advisory Board (AAB) and the Antiquities and Monuments Office (AMO) in Hong Kong provide are as follows:
GRADE 1: Buildings of outstanding merit; every effort should be made to preserve them, if possible.
GRADE 2: Buildings of special merit; efforts should be made to selectively preserve them.
GRADE 3: Buildings of some merit; preservation in some form would be desirable and alternative means could be considered if preservation is not practicable.
Graded historical buildings, however, do not have any statutory protection unless declared as monuments. In accordance with the Antiquities and Monuments Ordinance, the Antiquities Authority may, after consultation with the Antiquities Advisory Board and with the approval of the chief executive, and by notice in the *Gazette*, declare a place, building, site, or structure to be a monument. The Antiquities Authority is then empowered to prevent alterations, or to impose conditions upon any proposed alterations as it deems fit in order to protect the monument.

2 For additional information on *Demolition as Construction,* see the RAD website at http://www.rad.hk/projects/venice-biennale-2010-demolition-construction.

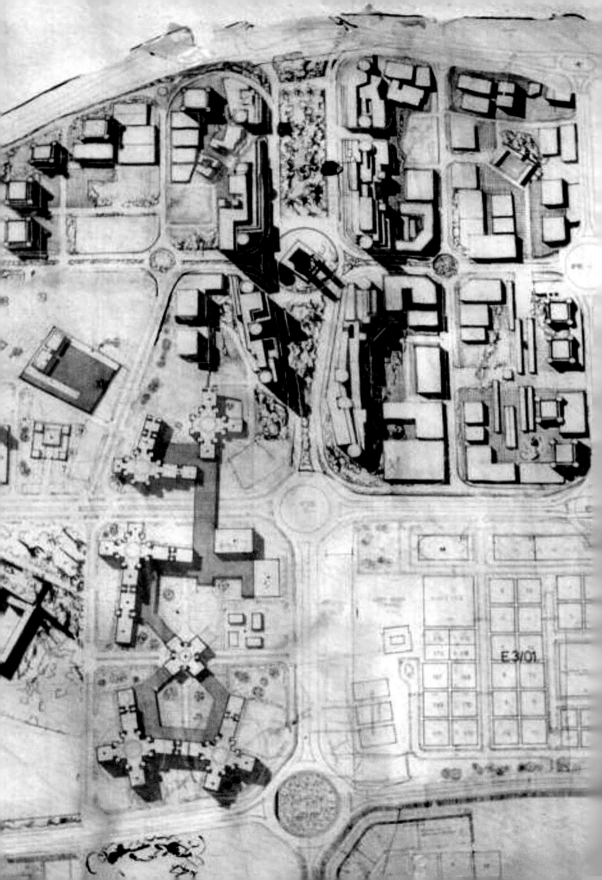

The Evolution of Abu Dhabi City's Urbanization and the Sustainability Challenge

KAIS SAMARRAI

INTRODUCTION

Abu Dhabi City is a capital with a grand vision for the future. It arose from a forgotten fishing village located in the harsh desert and coastal environments of the Arabian Peninsula to develop as a thriving urban center in the twenty-first century.
Urban planning and development have always played a key role in the economic and social development of Abu Dhabi City. This essay analyzes the evolution of its planning, highlighting key efforts and policies that have shaped this rapidly growing metropolis, and also examines some of the challenges that confront its aspirations.

BACKGROUND

Abu Dhabi Emirate is one of the seven emirates forming the United Arab Emirates (UAE), and Abu Dhabi City is the nation's capital. The emirate is located in the southeastern portion of the Arabian Peninsula, and shares a border with the Sultanate of Oman, the emirates of Dubai and Sharjah, and Saudi Arabia (FIG. 1). It occupies an area of 67,340 square kilometers, representing 87 percent of the UAE's total land area, and has a coastline of nearly seven hundred kilometers along the Arabian/Persian Gulf and more than two hundred natural islands. The emirate is divided into three administrative regions. The first is the Capital Region, which includes Abu Dhabi Island, smaller adjacent islands, and the landmass that extends to the borders of Dubai and that is known as the Abu Dhabi mainland. The second is the Eastern Region, with al-'Ain City as its main center. It is located near the edge of the Hajar Mountain range and is known for its oases and its limited agricultural activity. The third is the Western Region, which is defined by the expansive and resource-rich desert and shoreline. It has three main settlements: Madinat Zayed, al-Mirfa, and the industrial city of al-Ruwais. Almost 85 percent of the emirate's landmass is sand desert that extends to the Empty Quarter of the Arabian Peninsula, and another 7 percent is low-lying salt flats, or what is referred to in Arabic as *sabkha*. Moreover, 90 percent of the ground water in the Emirate of Abu Dhabi is

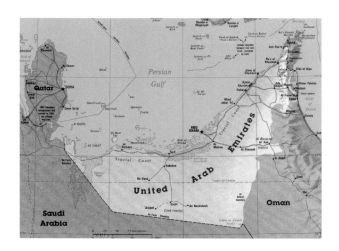

FIG. 1: Map of the United Arab Emirates.

FIG. 2: Aerial view of Abu Dhabi, 1954.

saline and unsuitable for drinking or for supporting any viable agriculture. In addition, the arid desert climate is characterized by temperatures that reach 48 degrees Celsius in the summer, and little rainfall during the short winters. Accordingly, although Abu Dhabi's desert and coastal areas are characterized by a rich level of biodiversity, 93 percent of its landmass is inhospitable to human habitation.

The population of Abu Dhabi Emirate grew exponentially from less than 20,000 people in 1960 to over 2,450,000 in 2013. Abu Dhabi City currently has a population of about 1,498,000, which amounts to nearly 61 percent of the emirate's total population.

THE PRE-OIL SETTLEMENT OF ABU DHABI ISLAND

Settlement in Abu Dhabi City dates back to 1871 when the tribes of the Bani Yas alliance decided to move from the Liwa desert oasis in the Western Region and settle in Abu Dhabi Island, which offered fresh groundwater and natural protection from the attacks of Al Saud from central Arabia who waged campaigns to control the Arabian Peninsula between 1765 and 1891. Their settlement gradually grew near the northern tip of the island, forming what appears as an organic and unplanned village (FIG. 2). An analysis of the urban form of the nineteen-fifties town, however, shows that it was organized according to functional necessities, a basic understanding of the natural environment, and unwritten cultural codes. The orientation of the streets and major open spaces followed the shoreline and took advantage of the prevailing winds to capture incoming sea breezes, and were north-facing to minimize exposure to the sun. The central area served as a commercial spine connecting the harbor with Qasr al-Husn, the dominating ruler's fort that was built in 1761 as a watchtower and later expanded in 1793 into a small fort. Residential quarters were connected through a hierarchy of pathways and open spaces, and each residential quarter, or *fareej,* as it was traditionally called, was occupied by a different tribe.

During the first half of the twentieth century, the Emirate of Abu Dhabi was focused on a small fishing village and was one of the least urbanized areas in the region. Other nearby cities such as Dubai, Sharjah, Muscat, and Manama were more developed, trade-based centers. With the exception of a few permanent structures, most of the population of Abu Dhabi Island lived in temporary huts made of palm branches, or what is known as *barasti* dwellings, and had to do without basic services, schools, or hospitals.

THE POST-OIL ERA (1962–2004)

In 1939, Sheikh Shakhbout bin Sultan Al Nahyan, the Ruler of Abu Dhabi, granted British Petroleum the first oil concessions in Abu Dhabi, but it was not until nineteen years later that they found commercially viable oil reserves, and oil exports did not start until 1962. The year 1961 marked the establishment of the Abu Dhabi Municipality, which was concerned with delivering key services such as drinking water and public health facilities. In addition to serving the immediate requirements of the town's four thousand residents, there also was a need to accommodate the growing working population that came about as a result of the presence of oil companies. In 1962, the government accordingly commissioned two British consultancy firms, Sir William Halcrow and Scott Wilson Kirkpatrick & Partners, to develop the first urban plan for Abu Dhabi City. Halcrow developed a plan that would ultimately accommodate one hundred thousand people, and proposed a first phase for twenty-five thousand people. Forecasted growth was based on the assumption that the main function of the city would be to serve the exploration and export of oil, benchmarking similar examples in North Africa. The plan also proposed dredging and reclamation work to improve maritime navigation in the shallow waters around Abu Dhabi Island. Roads were not completely straight, and were integrated into the existing settlement. This is in spite of the plan's recommendation that most of the settlement be removed and replaced by a new administrative area near the fort that is bordered by residential clusters. The plan designated new areas for the expansion of residential, recreation, and industrial areas (related to oil storage and export), a hospital, and a site for an airport. Five years after oil was first exported in 1962, however, residents saw very little improvement to their living conditions. Except for a lone desalination plant providing Abu Dhabi City with fresh water instead of the usual salty supply, no planned services were delivered. This was related to the fact that Sheikh Shakhbout did not trust the British, was wary of changes coming from the West, and was reluctant to use oil revenues.

It was not until 1966, when Sheikh Zayed bin Sultan Al Nahyan was chosen by the Al Nahyan family, with the help of the British, as the leader of Abu Dhabi that it began to undergo tangible changes, and public spending on development was initiated. The new ruler established new departments for public works, health, and education, and created a new municipality for al-'Ain. He also instructed a reevaluation and revision of the Halcrow Plan, and appointed Arabicon Associated Consultants, a consortium

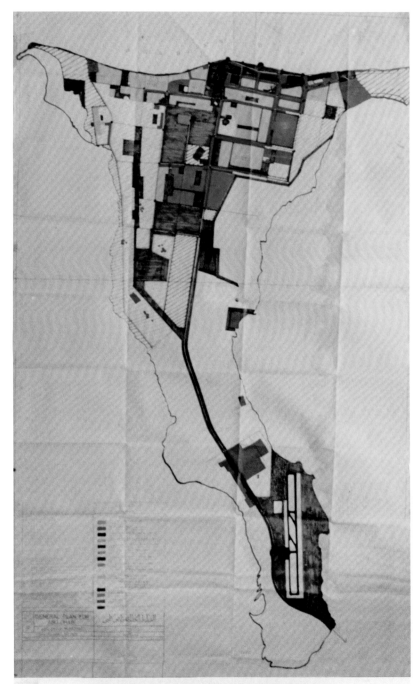

TAKAHASHI LAND USE PLAN FEB. 1968

Fɪɢ. 3: Abu Dhabi's "Takahashi Plan," 1968.

Fig. 4: Katsuhiko Takahashi presenting his plan to Sheikh Zayed bin Sultan Al Nahyan (LEFT), and a partial view of the plan (RIGHT).

of British consultants, to prepare detailed neighborhood plans. The new plan adopted a gridiron street pattern and proposed large blocks and wide roads with large roundabouts at intersections. Qasr al-Husn was kept, along with the location of old mosques, but the old settlement was removed and replaced by commercial and business districts, and owners were compensated with commercial, residential, and industrial plots. In 1967, the young Japanese architect and planner Katsuhiko Takahashi was appointed as chief town planner for Abu Dhabi Municipality. He expanded the Arabicon plans and delivered detailed designs for the plan's administrative and commercial buildings (FIGS. 3 AND 4). The influence of Arata Isozaki's 1960–61 utopian "City in the Sky" project seems apparent in Takahashi's proposed 1967 plans for the central governmental and commercial areas. Although what was implemented differed from what was proposed, the plan was the base for most planning efforts that followed.

During the nineteen-sixties and nineteen-seventies, Arab architects designed key buildings, such as al-Manhal Palace by Sayyid Kurayyim, the Grand Mosque by Hisham al-Huseini and Zaki al-Humsie, and housing projects by Midhat Ali Mathloum. Furthermore, international consultancy firms prepared new designs for al-Maqta' Bridge, the airport, and the port. The population of Abu Dhabi grew from four thousand to twenty-two thousand people between 1962 and 1968, and in 1968, the Planning Board was established by Sheikh Zayed to become the responsible authority to guide the emirate's development and growth. In order to ensure implementation of key developments in all sectors, a "Five Year Development Plan" was announced. In October of that year,

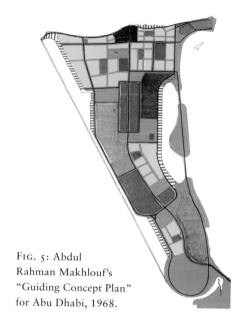

FIG. 5: Abdul
Rahman Makhlouf's
"Guiding Concept Plan"
for Abu Dhabi, 1968.

the Abu Dhabi Municipality appointed Abdul Rahman Makhlouf as the city's new chief town planner. He later became the director of the newly created Town Planning Department within the municipality. Prior to Abu Dhabi, he had worked in Jeddah and Medina in Saudi Arabia. Being an Egyptian and a native speaker of Arabic gave him an immediate advantage in terms of understanding the culture of the place.

Makhlouf embraced the Arabicon and Takahashi plans and expanded them according to the guidance of the ruler. The improved plan was referred to as the "Guiding Concept Plan," which implies that the plan was adaptable and would accommodate the leadership's directions and emerging needs (FIGS. 5 AND 6). Sheikh Zayed initiated, directed, and closely monitored planning and development until his death in 2004. He was involved in both strategic and detailed planning decisions, from prioritizing projects and selecting consultants to deciding street widths and plot sizes.

FIG. 6: Makhlouf presenting his plan to Sheikh Zayed, 1975.

FIG. 7: Aerial view of Abu Dhabi, 1970.

THE GENESIS OF ABU DHABI'S URBAN FORM

The earlier plans for Abu Dhabi City embraced the dominant planning doctrines of the modern automobile-oriented cities of the nineteen-sixties. The commercial sectors of Abu Dhabi Island were planned with wide roads and boulevards, large rectangular super blocks with lengths of one kilometer in some instances, medians with lush trees, grand roundabouts, and sizeable public parks (FIG. 7). The lower half of the island was dedicated to low-density single-family residential dwellings. The morphology and urban form of Abu Dhabi City, however, was not only influenced by the late nineteen-sixties planning decisions. It was also driven by the social welfare policy of equitable plot allocation and distribution to help generate steady streams of income for citizens through renting out properties to expatriates. The sizes of the plots and building heights were regulated to give owners the same development rights. Most commercial plot sizes were between 25 meters by 15 meters and 30 meters by 30 meters. Today, a typical commercial city block facing a main street may be occupied by a twenty- to twenty-four-story building, in contrast to eight to ten stories in the nineteen-seventies. An inner block may contain six-story low-rise buildings or two-story villas with surface parking. Exceptions to these rules exist for special blocks with landmark buildings or developments such as the Baynuna Towers, the Abu Dhabi World Trade Center, and the Abu Dhabi Investment Authority headquarters.

Another factor accounting for this uniformity and repetitiveness of urban form is the role of the Khalifa Committee, named after the current ruler of Abu Dhabi and president of the UAE. The committee was established in 1977, when Sheikh Khalifa bin Zayed was crown prince, to help citizens develop, finance, design, contract, and manage the commercial plots bestowed on them in exchange for a small share of the returns. Over two hundred apartment blocks were constructed every year during the nineteen-eighties and nineteen-nineties. The committee influenced the design of the buildings to control costs. This brought about functional but bland results. Quantity often trumped quality (FIG. 8).

THE MAKING OF "SUBURBARABIA"

Sheikh Zayed's primary objective during the early days of planned growth was to settle the emirate's nomadic tribes within cities. As for those who could not be lured to urban living and to mixing with outsiders, they would be provided with all necessary services and settled in suburbs and in rural areas. The Abu Dhabi Public Works Department built thousands of houses known as *sha'biyyat* for them during the first decade of Sheikh Zayed's reign. Families from the same tribe were housed close to each other—a practice that was later abandoned in large settlements in order to avoid social problems related to tribal loyalties, and to foster a national identity. These houses for nationals were built on large plots with ample open space, or, in some cases, with farmland offered to initiate a transition from nomadic to suburban living. The size of a single-family plot size, however, was

FIG. 8: View of typical city blocks in Abu Dhabi showing the uniformity of building typologies and heights, 2009.

reduced to forty-five by forty-five meters in 1995. A number of suburban townships also were developed about twenty-five to fifty kilometers outside the main island between the late-nineteen-seventies and mid-nineteen-nineties, along the freeways to al-'Ain and Dubai. These included the townships of Bani Yas, al-Shahama, al-Samha, al-Rahba, and al-Bahya. Schools, mosques, and hospitals were provided for these developments, but most communities lacked public transport amenities and parks, as well as recreational and retail services. National housing projects continue to shape the growth boundaries of the city and to fuel suburban sprawl to this day.

THE UNION

The successful union of the seven Trucial States to form the UAE in 1971 following British withdrawal from the Gulf boosted the regional prominence of Abu Dhabi City since it became the capital of the new nation. The city's new political and symbolic role needed to be reflected and represented in physical form and through tangible urban, economic, and social improvements. An exponential pace of development accordingly marked the city during the nineteen-seventies and nineteen-eighties, and this continued throughout the nineteen-nineties. The population of Abu Dhabi City grew from about twenty-two thousand to over half a million inhabitants between 1968 and 2001, and the area covered by urbanization expanded from 272 to 9,000 hectares.

Despite this rapid urbanization, there was a consciousness of the need to maintain a balance between modernizing the city and protecting its traditional Arab identity. The designs of numerous buildings accordingly were commisioned to Arab architects including Rifat Chadirji, who designed the Abu Dhabi National Theater in 1977, Jafar Tukan, who designed the Ministry of Finance building in 1979, 'Abbad al-Radi and Nizar Ahmed, who designed the Fish Market in 1992, and Hisham Ashkouri who designed the Cultural Foundation Complex in 1977. Additionally, a few foreign architectural offices worked on developing examples of modern regional architecture such as the French architect Henri Colboc, who designed the Zayed Sport City in 1979. Some of Abu Dhabi's best modern architectural heritage belongs to this era extending from the nineteen-seventies to the nineteen-nineties.

THE 1990–2010 ABU DHABI COMPREHENSIVE MASTER PLAN

Between 1989 and 1991, the Abu Dhabi Government commenced preparations for a comprehensive development master plan for the emirate. It was the first long-term regional plan for the emirate, and was led by the Abu Dhabi City Town Planning Department and the United Nations Development Programme (UNDP), in collaboration

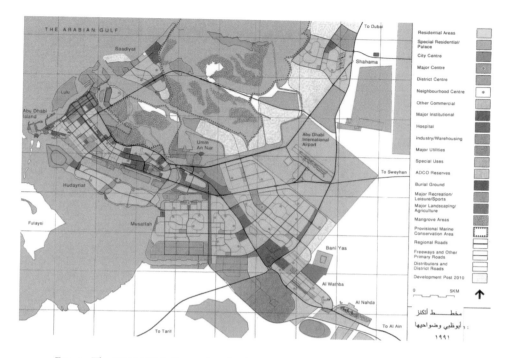

FIG. 9: The 1990–2010 Comprehensive Master Plan for Abu Dhabi, prepared by the
Abu Dhabi City Town Planning Department and the United Nations Development Programme
(UNDP), with the international engineering firm Atkins as consultants, 1990.

with the international engineering firm Atkins, who acted as consultants. The plan
provided an extensive detailed analysis of environmental and socioeconomic conditions in the emirate. It also offered an in-depth analysis of housing and of the real
estate market, and stressed the need to reform the real estate sector. In addition, its
final document provided "Master Directive Plans" for Abu Dhabi City and all adjacent
settlements, including those in the Western Region, covering the emirate's urbanization framework and land use along with an execution plan. For Abu Dhabi City, the
plan suggested three growth options outlined in the "Master Directive Plan for Abu
Dhabi and its Environs." The growth option eventually chosen allowed for the expansion of the existing city to the neighboring islands of al-Saadiyat, al-Hodariyat, and
al-Reem, in addition to allowing growth towards the mainland along the highways to
Dubai and al-'Ain. The plan identified future highway corridors connecting the islands
and also identified land uses in a manner that minimized impact on sensitive coastal
environments (FIG. 9).

At the policy level, the plan recommended a number
of reforms that included the following:

- Create a national "Five Year Plan" for economic and social development.
- Address the different housing preferences of nationals and expatriate populations, and provide them with the needed community facilities.
- Allow the land to be sold, and reform existing land allocation practices that took place at higher levels of government and that were not always in accordance with planned growth, as this resulted in an inefficient utilization of land and in urban sprawl.
- Review plot sizes in the central area and allow the merging of small plots to meet the need for larger ones and to accommodate more functional layouts.
- Prepare local plans and improve urban design practices and design quality as well as building quality and maintenance.
- Update existing rigid building regulations to allow for more flexibility to accommodate future needs for different land uses.

A decade after the adoption of the plan, many of its important components still were not followed or implemented. For instance, large residential developments spread south of Abu Dhabi Airport, beyond the limit of growth set by the master plan, and the al-Mussafah area remained an industrial one and was not developed into a residential area as planned. Also, the plan specified that the site of al-Bateen Airport near the southeastern end of Abu Dhabi Island would become the district for the federal government and for minstries, but this was abandoned. Multimodal public transport plans were not pursued, the bridge that was to link Abu Dhabi City to al-Saadiyat Island was later constructed in a different location, and only one of the three conections to al-Hodariyat Island was executed, as the island itself remained undeveloped. The plan also recommended a number of important projects to be considered for Abu Dhabi as a capital city, but none of them were pursued. These include a national museum, a national public library, and a landmark public square.

FOOTLOOSE URBAN DEVELOPMENT

For decades, urban development in Abu Dhabi was centralized and managed by the government. Moreover, ownership of land and properties was restricted to UAE nationals. Following the death of Sheikh Zayed in 2004, the emirate's new young and Western-educated leadership sought to open up the economy to adapt to new global and regional changes that took place following the September 11, 2001 attacks and the United States' invasion of Iraq in 2003. The fears of retribution by American lawmakers targeting Gulf investors in the United States directed a good portion of their investments back from the United States to the Gulf region. Concurrently, oil prices rose in 2004 to surpass $50 a barrel, and this trend continued until the price peaked at $140 in 2008. The result was an accumulation of sizable reserves in local banks that could be used to finance various projects. Compelled by its diminishing oil resources, the business-friendly neighboring Emirate of Dubai was ready to take advantage of such new economic opportunities, and declared its ambition to become a global city. Its unprecedented themed real estate projects, including its gigantic manmade islands and lavish malls, gained Dubai worldwide attention.

The year 2005 brought a significant shift to the real estate market in Abu Dhabi. For the first time, private property development companies were authorized to hold and develop land, and foreign investment was allowed in designated "investment zones." In addition, nationals were permitted to sell government bestowed land. Because of its considerable wealth, the opening of Abu Dhabi's real estate market to investment (which up to that time had been closed and relatively protected from speculation) attracted many investors, both local and international.

Numerous property development companies were soon established. These included Aldar, Tamouh, Sorouh, Reem, Hydra, Manazel, and Al Qudra, to name a few. Most of these, if not all, are characterized by a level of government ownership. In fact, Mubadala Development Company, the investment and economic development arm of the state of Abu Dhabi, and the Tourism Development and Investment Company (TDIC) are fully government-owned development companies with specific mandates to help achieve strategic economic objectives. All these companies were granted significant plots of land to develop in and around Abu Dhabi City.

Not to be outshined by neighboring Dubai, numerous megaprojects were announced in Abu Dhabi in 2005 and 2006. These projects included the cultural district in al-Saadiyat Island with branded museums including the Louvre and the Guggenheim; the Yas Island development by Aldar Properties, which was branded with the Ferrari World theme park and the Formula 1 race circuit; al-Raha Beach mixed-use development; Masdar City as the world's first zero-carbon city; and al-Reem Island, the biggest commercial development in Abu Dhabi to date. These five projects alone are designed to accommodate nearly six hundred thousand people when fully developed. Almost all these themed megaprojects are not in line with the 1990–2010 Abu Dhabi Comprehensive Master Plan since they are either located outside the planned growth areas or do not conform to specified land uses and densities. The leadership of Abu Dhabi in fact soon realized that urban development had to be controlled, regulated, and channeled to serve the economic and social development goals set forth for the emirate.

A POLICY SHIFT

The call for the need to diversify Abu Dhabi's economic base and to reduce its heavy reliance on its ample hydrocarbon resources first emerged in the recommendations set forth in the 1990–2010 Abu Dhabi Comprehensive Master Plan. The economic experts of the Executive Affairs Authority (EAA) have repeated this call since its establishment in 2006 to ensure the long-term resilience and financial security of the emirate. Chaired by the CEO of Mubadala, the EAA is an advisory agency to the chairman of the Abu Dhabi Executive Council on strategic policies across all sectors of government. It has been a driving force behind restructuring the Abu Dhabi government and diversifying its economy. Mubadala was created as the "principal agent" for the delivery of this strategic objective with direct investment in key social, economic, and technological sectors.

The Abu Dhabi Council for Economic Development (ADCED) was established in 2006 "to facilitate economic diversification and growth through creating greater understanding, cooperation, and engagement between public and private sectors." The vision is to establish a "world-class" economic hub with sustainable growth, and to develop the human capital of Abu Dhabi. The sustainability objective was both a choice and a necessity. The leadership of Abu Dhabi recognized that fossil fuel resources are finite and that it would be wise to invest in alternative energy and income sources while Abu Dhabi has the financial means to support this transition. Oil prices are also volatile and can potentially put the economy at risk. Additionally, it became evident that with ongoing rates of urbanization and population growth, the cost of subsidizing energy and water—now reaching $4.76 billion annually—cannot be sustained indefinitely. Moreover, Abu Dhabi sought to differentiate itself from its neighbors, namely Dubai, by choosing the path of sustainability, which has become an integral part of Abu Dhabi's branding campaign.

As a response to immense real estate development pressures, it was evident that the existing urban plans needed to be reexamined. Therefore, under the direction of Sheikh Mohammed bin Zayed Al Nahyan, the Chairman of the Abu Dhabi Executive Council and the Crown Prince of the UAE, a new Urban Structure Framework Plan was prepared and published in 2007 to accommodate and control urban growth and to facilitate the efficient spatial distribution of infrastructure and economic activities. Along with the plan, a new law was announced in 2007 to establish a new independent government agency with a broad mandate, the Abu Dhabi Urban Planning Council (UPC), to govern the emirate's urban growth.

The adoption of this new urban planning vision in 2007, prior to the completion of the Abu Dhabi Economic Vision 2030 (see below) in 2008, shows the important role given to urban development in achieving Abu Dhabi's economic transformation in a manner that allows it to reach its global ambitions. The economic and developmental vision for Abu Dhabi sets the year 2030 as the milestone for transforming it into a "dynamic, open, and sustainable global economy."

PLAN ABU DHABI 2030:
THE URBAN STRUCTURE FRAMEWORK PLAN

The Urban Structure Framework Plan was prepared between December 2006 and September 2007 to serve as a conceptual guiding document for the urban growth of Abu Dhabi City over the following two decades, and to lay the foundation for a future comprehensive plan. Economic analysis and demographic projections were prepared by two international consultancies, the Boston Consulting Group and Economic Research Associates, and both expected the population of the Abu Dhabi City region to reach three million or more by 2030. Unlike the 1990–2010 Comprehensive Master Plan, the 2007 Framework Plan excluded the Eastern and the Western regions and focused on the Capital City region. Nevertheless, the rich and detailed studies carried out for the previous plan, which covers the historical and cultural context, environmental aspects, varying housing demands, settlement patterns, and the analysis of the built form of the inner city, proved to be highly relevant and extremely beneficial in formulating the new plan. Additionally, a number of high-level studies, surveys, and reviews were conducted to assess existing plans and policies related to infrastructure, environment, transportation, cultural values, and worker housing, as well as evaluating some of the major aforementioned proposed developments.

Two charrettes were carried out under the direct supervision of the Crown Prince of Abu Dhabi that involved local and international experts as well as government officials from different agencies. The outcomes included an environmental framework, the formation of growth scenarios, and the articulation of guiding principles to evaluate growth options. The overarching principles for the plan focused on a number of themes that address the identity of Abu Dhabi City as a contemporary Arab capital. It also specified that Abu Dhabi is to grow in a "measured" and sustainable manner while protecting its natural environment, and that the "urban fabric and community infrastructure will enable the values, social arrangements, culture, and mores of this Arab community." Urban growth options were illustrated in the form of maps and diagrams that translated the plan's principles into a spatial form that showed the distribution of densities, land uses, transportation infrastructure, and public open spaces. More detailed plans were prepared for special districts. The preservation of Abu Dhabi's unique coastal and desert environments was also emphasized. The plan analyzed the "building block" of the Emirati settlements and offered optimal patterns that could be applied to small communities, urban areas, and central business districts, as well as patterns for desert or island eco-villages (FIG. 10). The most significant outcome of the options that the plan considered was the creation of a new capital center on the mainland that was called the "Capital District," but that has since been renamed "Zayed City," and that is located twenty-five kilometers from the traditional Abu Dhabi City Central Business District (CBD). The capital center will be the seat of the federal government, but will also contain a university, a high-tech research precinct, and embassies, in addition to a hospital, a stadium, mixed-used commercial and

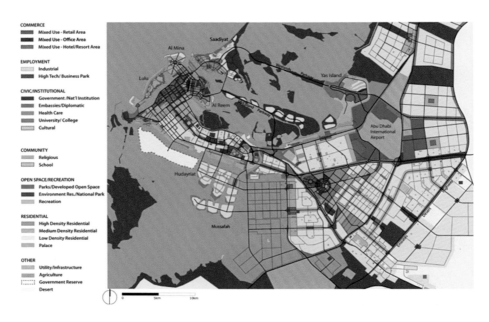

FIG. 10: Plan Abu Dhabi 2030, Land Use Plan, prepared by the Boston Consulting Group and Economic Research Associates, 2007.

retail centers, and a large Emirati residential low-density neighborhood (FIGS. 11 AND 12). The Capital District covers about 4,900 hectares with a planned capacity of more than three hundred and fifty thousand people. However, the Plan Abu Dhabi 2030 update in November 2013, which was led by UPC, scaled back the population projection for Abu Dhabi City to 2.4 million by 2030. It is accordingly expected that Zayed City's population will be proportionately scaled back as well.

The idea of creating a new government center of this scale has both supporters and critics.

FIG. 11: Plan Abu Dhabi 2030, Zayed City (The Capital District), plan, 2007.

Fig. 12: Plan Abu Dhabi 2030, Zayed City
(The Capital District), aerial view, 2007.

Supporters see it as vital to providing jobs outside the congested island by bringing the government and federal district closer to Emirati suburban communities in Greater Abu Dhabi City and the rest of the UAE. It would also create a strong identity worthy of the nation's capital. Critics, however, suggest that building a new center twenty-five kilometers from the traditional CBD would weaken the existing CBD and the planned financial center on al-Maryah Island. In addition, heavy reliance on personal cars would continue since connecting the new Capital District to rapid transit systems may not be feasible due to the sizable distance between the two centers and the low population densities in between. Still, creating new centers closer to Emirati communities is of great importance. The scale and phasing of the new centers have to be carefully tied to economic and population growth, and they should be efficiently served by public transportation and other necessary amenities.

TRANSPORTATION PLANNING

Regarding transportation, Plan Abu Dhabi 2030 praised Abu Dhabi's grid system, and highlighted the importance of achieving a balanced land use distribution. It, however, also stressed the need to develop a multimodal transit system that includes metro, light rail, and regional rail systems, and discouraged the development of freeways. It also advised enhancing connectivity within the super blocks in the inner city, and underlined the importance of improving the pedestrian experience and safety as well as the need to address car-parking deficiencies.

The Department of Transport interpreted the strategies of the transportation framework outlined in the Plan Abu Dhabi 2030 and completed the Abu Dhabi Surface Transport Master Plan (ADSTMP) in 2009. The provision of transportation infrastructure was based on anticipated land uses and densities set by Plan Abu Dhabi 2030. A number of key road infrastructure projects have been delivered to connect newly developed communities and destinations. Public transportation plans for light rail and metro networks have been delayed, but are still under development and revisions.

In contrast, Etihad Rail, the $11 billion regional rail project connecting the Abu Dhabi Emirate from the Saudi border to al-Fujaira Port on the Arabian Sea has made significant progress and is due for completion in 2018. It is the first regional rail project in the Gulf region and can potentially connect the countries of the Gulf Cooperation Council through freight and passenger rail in the future.

THE URBAN PLANNING COUNCIL (UPC) AND *ESTIDAMA*

The UPC's stated role is to manage the emirate's sustainable urban growth through the planning of appropriate infrastructure while preserving the environment and the equitable distribution of economic activities, enhancing Abu Dhabi's urban fabric, and providing social and cultural infrastructure for Emirati communities. The UPC is also responsible for developing plans, regulations, guidelines, and policies relating to urban planning. In addition, it reviews all major and strategic public and private development projects in order to ensure that sustainability principals are integrated, and to warrant the alignment of development projects with governmental plans and policies.

In 2008, the UPC started developing a major sustainability initiative called *Estidama*—the Arabic word for sustainability—to encourage sustainable growth and development. The concept is based on four pillars: environmental, economic, social, and cultural sustainability. The last was included to emphasize the unique cultural values and heritage of Abu Dhabi. Estidama is also a rating system for communities and buildings that is carefully crafted to respond to the specific challenges of the region, namely the conservation of water and energy. Beginning in 2010, satisfying the Estidama rating system became a mandatory requirement for all new developments in the Abu Dhabi Emirate. Moreover, government buildings, mosques, and schools have been required to surpass the minimum sustainability rating. To ensure the sustainability of all upcoming infrastructure work, the UPC issued the new Urban Street Design Manual and the Utility Corridor Design Manual to optimize the sizes of infrastructure works and minimize the unnecessary waste of land, and to improve the quality of urban streets. This effort was followed by the release of the Public Realm Design Manual, the Community Facilities Standards, and the Safety and Security Planning Manual. Estidama requirements were integrated with all such standards and manuals to generate the concept of "Complete Sustainable Communities."

The shift towards sustainability and high-quality urban design has been implemented through the evaluation of all major projects using an integrated and multidisciplinary review process by the UPC and in coordination with all stakeholders. New developments are now being built according to the new standards and are gradually making a noticeable difference. It may take some time, however, before the impact of the new standards on the existing city becomes apparent. Moreover, these same standards also need to be applied to a revitalization effort for the inner city.

MASDAR CITY

In parallel to these planning efforts in 2006, Abu Dhabi launched the Masdar City initiative as the world's first totally sustainable development, and the Masdar Institute of Science and Technology (MIST), which is dedicated entirely to sustainability and energy research. The six-square-kilometer development is located in the desert near the Abu Dhabi International Airport and the new Capital District, and is expected to accommo-

FIG. 13: Masdar City, Abu Dhabi, Foster + Partners, aerial view, 2006.

date forty thousand residents and fifty thousand employees when completed (FIG. 13). The initial plan of Masdar City, which was prepared by the British-based architectural firm Foster + Partners, was inspired by the traditional urban solutions of Arab cities. The plan integrates passive design techniques (that is, compact built form, short and narrow streets, and suitable building orientation to maximize shading and wind movement), the use of renewable energy sources, and an efficient sophisticated infrastructure. Construction began in 2008, and the first phase of the development, which includes the Masdar Institute buildings and student residences, the Siemens headquarters, the Incubator office building, and the International Renewable Energy Agency (IRENA) headquarters are operational. The city currently generates its energy needs from the largest photovoltaic power station in the Middle East. During the last few years of its operation, there has been a great deal of learning and experimentation with technological solutions that were tested on the ground. Among the lessons learned is the realization that conventional photovoltaic panels are not efficient in the desert environment because of the easy accumulation of sand. Accordingly, advanced panels are under development to overcome this limitation. The city development team also realized that it is more feasible to construct future phases of the development on the ground rather than continuing with the practice of raising the city on a podium. Consequently, the high-tech Personal Rapid Transport (PRT) system currently operating under the podium will be replaced by an alternative system connected to Abu Dhabi City's future metro and light rail network. Additionally, the revised plan will allow electric cars and delivery vehicles to enter the city in contrast to the initial plan, which kept automobiles at the city's boundaries.

In spite of the criticism that has appeared over the last decade regarding Masdar's heavy reliance on technological solutions, its social exclusion, and the limited public participation involved in its making, Masdar City still represents a profound urban experiment offering a comprehensive approach to how future cities may be developed to successfully address the pillars of sustainability: environmental protection, economic opportunity, and bringing about social and cultural improvements for local communities. Masdar City is playing a key role in the transformation of Abu Dhabi's economy and urban living from a carbon dependent to a sustainable one with a strong knowledge and innovation base.

THE CHALLENGES AHEAD AND CONCLUSION

The urban evolution of Abu Dhabi City has been a remarkable story that has extended from the humble beginnings of a fishing village to a thriving capital with global ambitions. Urban development has always played a major role in the economic development of Abu Dhabi City. Planning for the rapid growth of the city during the nineteen-seventies, eighties, and nineties was driven by a strong governmental social welfare agenda, and was funded by the influx of wealth generated from oil exports. The post-2004 policy shift, which has aimed at enabling the transition of Abu Dhabi City from a conservative regional city to a global one with a sustainable and diversified economy, has brought new opportunities and many challenges. The fundamental challenge for planners and regulators is to achieve a balance between economic development objectives and environmental, social, and cultural sustainability. Although the economic benefits of globalization and urban development have contributed to the prosperity and wealth of the citizens of Abu Dhabi, the long-term social and environmental cost of continued growth has not been evaluated.

One result of the constant expansion of economic activities has been an increased demographic imbalance, which is a major planning and social challenge for Abu Dhabi, and also for other cities in the Gulf region. The population disparity between migrant workers and the native population is strongly evident as expatriates currently amount to 80 percent of the total population in the Emirate of Abu Dhabi.

Abu Dhabi has made notable progress in the diversification of its economy through increased investment in infrastructure, real estate development, tourism, and finance. In addition, Abu Dhabi's vision for the future aims to achieve a transition towards a knowledge-based economy and towards becoming an innovation hub. Investing in human capital and attracting world-class universities and technological institutions such as New York University, Sorbonne University, and the Masdar Institute of Technology—with its close affiliation to the Massachusetts Institute of Technology (MIT), and Masdar City—are among the steps that have been taken in implementing this transition. However, according to the Knowledge Economy Index (KEI), an indicator set by the World Bank Knowledge Assessment Methodology (KAM), despite making considerable advancements in information and communications infrastructure, the UAE needs to make improvements in innovation systems, and education and skills, as well as economic and institutional development.

Greater investments in research and development (R&D) can lead to a faster transition to a knowledge-based economy and may correct this demographic imbalance. The annual expenditure on R&D in the UAE between 2005 and 2012, however, was equivalent to 0.49% of its GDP, which is significantly below the international average of 2.13%.

Abu Dhabi has made great progress in articulating its sustainability vision, policies, and initiatives, and can move quickly towards detailing them into comprehensive and adaptable plans with clear implementation programs. Important urban strategies may be explored to ensure sustainable growth. These include the densification of Abu Dhabi Island instead of expanding development beyond the urban growth boundaries, combined with implementing an efficient multimodal rapid transit system. Additionally, the revitalization of the inner city and the CBD as part of a larger capital investment plan is vital to presenting Abu Dhabi City as a livable and vibrant city with a distinct identity. Finally, supporting the Masdar City development will be an important component in Abu Dhabi's long-term urban and economic transformation towards a sustainable future.

Abu Dhabi has the potential to demonstrate that a bigger city or a bigger economy is not necessarily better. The implementation of the Abu Dhabi Economic Vision 2030 can allow it to emerge as a prosperous, resilient, and a world-class sustainable city.

ADDITIONAL READING:

For information on the geography, history, and urban development of Abu Dhabi, see the following:

Abu Dhabi Municipality and Town Planning Department, *Abu Dhabi Comprehensive Development Plan, Technical Report 1*. Abu Dhabi, 1991.

——. *Abu Dhabi, Dana of the Gulf*. Abu Dhabi, 2003.

Al-Fahim, Mohammed. *From Rags to Riches: A Story of Abu Dhabi*. London, 1998.

Elsheshtawy, Yasser, ed. *The Evolving Arab City: Tradition, Modernity and Urban Development*. London, 2008.

Ghazal, Rym. "The Man Behind Abu Dhabi's Master Plan." *The National*, November 11, 2013, http://www.thenational.ae/uae/heritage/the-man-behind-abu-dhabis-master-plan#full.

Lau, Arthur. "Masdar City: A Model of Urban Environmental Sustainability." *Nikhil Manghnani International Journal of Engineering Research and Applications* 4, no. 10 (October 2012).

Makhlouf, Abdul Rahman. "Abu Dhabi Town Before the Oil Production Era." Lecture delivered at the Tourist Club in Abu Dhabi, 1994.

Reiche, Danyel. "Renewable Energy Policies in the Gulf Countries: A Case Study of the Carbon-neutral 'Masdar City' in Abu Dhabi." *Energy Policy* 38, no. 1 (2009).

Statistic Centre Abu Dhabi (SCAD), http://www.scad.ae/en/statistics/Pages/Statistics.aspx?ThemeID=4.

Tok, Evren et al. "Crafting Smart Cities in the Gulf Region: A Comparison of Masdar and Lusail." *European Scientific Journal*, vol. 2 (June 2014).

Regarding developments specifically affecting planning in Abu Dhabi since 2004, see the following:

Abu Dhabi Council for Economic Development, *Abu Dhabi Economic Vision 2030*. Abu Dhabi, 2008.

Abu Dhabi Urban Planning Council, *Plan Abu Dhabi 2030*. Abu Dhabi, 2007.

Abu Dhabi Urban Planning Council, *Urban Structure Framework Plan 2030*. Abu Dhabi, 2007.

Mubadala's official website: https://www.mubadala.com/.

Masdar's official website: http://www.masdar.ae/.

Planning for Sustainable Growth in Singapore

LIM ENG HWEE

View of the walkway at Cloud Forest, Gardens by the Bay,
Singapore (LEFT).

SINGAPORE'S EXPERIENCE WITH EARLY URBANIZATION

Singapore was an emerging city in the nineteen-sixties. Most of its urban population was crowded in the city center under poor living conditions. There was an acute housing shortage, high unemployment, and inadequate infrastructure for transport, water, and sanitation. The focus for urban renewal then was to quickly improve its residents' living environment, fulfill basic housing needs, create employment for a rapidly growing population, and build a sense of belonging. With improved urban conditions, Singapore could attract more investment and support economic growth. Considering its lack of natural resources and a predominantly urban population, Singapore chose to create employment through industrialization, moving gradually over the decades from labor-intensive manufacturing sectors to high-tech, high value-added industries. We planned for the renewal

and long-term expansion of the city center to support Singapore's growth as a financial and business hub, and catered for an expansion of key infrastructure projects including the port, airport, and rapid transit lines.

Considering the pressing need to provide better housing for those living in overcrowded urban slum areas, we embarked on an extensive public housing program, and developed high-rise and self-sufficient towns around the island to accommodate the growing need for affordable housing. We prioritized the provision of greenery at the onset of our city planning endeavors with the launch of the Garden City campaign in 1967. The campaign sought to ensure that even as Singapore urbanized, development would be complemented with parks and greenery to provide shade and visual relief to the urban landscape, as well as clean air. Green spaces are provided as essential recreational, leisure, and social facilities. This is achieved not just through creating parks and setting aside land as nature reserves and areas,[1] but also through intensive planting along highways and streets, and within developments.

In a short span of fifty years, these efforts have enabled Singapore to develop into a modern city with a diversified, growing economy and with a significant presence in services (financial and insurance services, logistics, information communications technology (ICT), and tourism), manufacturing (electronics and chemicals), biomedical sciences, and engineering. Singapore also has consistently ranked high in international surveys on livability such as the Asian Green City Index and the Mercer Quality of Living Report.[2]

A LONG-TERM AND HOLISTIC FRAMEWORK FOR SUSTAINABLE GROWTH

Singapore is a small city-state occupying an area of 718 square kilometers with no natural resources. It still has to support an entire spectrum of needs that range from providing housing, parks, and community facilities to allocating land for industries, water catchment areas, defense facilities, ports, and airports. It is therefore important that a holistic and long-term land use planning approach is taken to provide for both current and future needs. This is to ensure that Singapore is able to achieve sustainable growth—whether socially, economically, or environmentally—that provides jobs and creates good quality living conditions in an environmentally responsible manner.

STRATEGIES FOR ECONOMIC SUSTAINABILITY

To ensure economic sustainability, we at the Urban Redevelopment Authority (URA) consider how our land may cater to future economic growth and a resilient economy, and also how to ensure that growth is inclusive, and consequently benefits the general population. As a country without a large hinterland, we are forced by necessity to be efficient, comprehensive, and detailed in our urban planning. We take a long-term view to ensure that we can achieve our strategic goals while building in an element of resiliency in order to respond to rapid geopolitical and economic changes.

It is critical for Singapore to remain relevant as a global city so as to attract investment and to create good job opportunities. This requires an open economy that is attractive to capital and knowledge investments, as well as land with the capacity to support continued growth in different economic sectors, whether services or manufacturing.

We plan ahead and safeguard sufficient land for diverse economic activities in manufacturing and services. For instance, we planned for the reclamation of Jurong Island for petrochemical industries, and set aside the mixed-use One North precinct for biomedical sciences, information and communications technology, and media activities, as well as the physical science and engineering sectors, and designated the Seletar Aerospace Park for aerospace industries. We have also created new synergies by clustering complementary uses such as high-technology corridors with business park developments and tertiary education institutions.

As early as the nineteen-sixties, Singapore's leadership had anticipated the growth of its Central Business District (CBD). To support Singapore's growth as a financial and business hub, Marina Bay was planned as a seamless extension of the CBD. Planning and land reclamation for Marina Bay began in the nineteen-seventies, with a number of new developments implemented in the past decade. It is due to this forward planning approach that the vision for a sustainable high-density and vibrant mixed-use, "24/7 live-work-play" district has taken shape.

At the same time, employment centers have been developed across the island in the form of regional, subregional, and fringe centers. This planning strategy has helped bring jobs closer to homes, reduce congestion and travel times, and provide affordable locations for businesses that do not need to be located in the CBD. Successful examples include the Tampines Regional Center, the Novena Fringe Center, One North, and the Changi Business Park.

More of such growth is now taking shape in the Jurong Lake District and Paya Lebar Central with the establishment of employment centers. Under the Master Plan 2014, we will focus on developing the North Coast Innovation Corridor, which will extend from the

Woodlands Regional Center to Punggol.[3] It will consist of integrated mixed-use developments providing a diverse mix of residences, recreational amenities, and commercial, business, and educational facilities. Punggol North will be home to a new integrated work-learn cluster comprising Singapore's fifth university, the Singapore Institute of Technology (SIT), as well as a new creative industry cluster for JTC, Singapore's lead agency entrusted with spearheading the planning, promotion, and development of an industrial landscape. The university will be the first to be developed in the heart of a public housing town, and the local community will share the use of SIT's facilities. Furthermore, to foster synergies, innovation, and collaboration between the academic community and industry, the SIT campus at Punggol North will be seamlessly integrated with JTC's new creative industry cluster. Students will be able to go from classroom to workplace, where they are able to apply what they've learned. As part of Singapore's first eco-town, the Punggol North precinct will also leverage district-wide systems such as district cooling and new smart technologies to achieve greater levels of environmental sustainability.

While more employment centers are being built outside the city center, there is growing demand for core financial and business service activities in the city center due to its prestigious location, good connectivity, and potential synergies with other businesses. To strengthen Singapore's status as a global hub for financial and business services, there is a need to continue providing sufficient high-quality commercial space within the city center while concurrently introducing more housing in and around the city center so that more people are able to enjoy the benefits of living near where they work. For example, Marina South is envisaged to be a lively mixed-use residential district that will provide about nine thousand new homes.[4]

STRATEGIES FOR SOCIAL SUSTAINABILITY

Providing a good quality of life for all is crucial to ensuring social sustainability. Therefore, the emphasis in Singapore is on providing sufficient housing, amenities, and recreation to meet its population's needs, while enhancing its character and sense of identity. When catering for housing needs, we seek to meet diverse requirements by safeguarding land for a variety of housing types and settings, ranging from affordable public housing to city and waterfront living. In addition, mixed-use housing towns are planned to include a wide range of amenities and facilities such as commercial, educational, healthcare, transport, recreational, leisure, and sports facilities that are easily accessible so as to create an inclusive living environment.

To cater to the different needs of residents and achieve greater community interaction, it is important to co-locate different types of community facilities, provide elderly-friendly and intergenerational spaces near housing, as well as provide common public spaces for different types of activities.

There is also an emphasis on balancing urban development with the need to preserve local identity and livability by planning for the rejuvenation of towns and estates under the Housing and Development Board's (HDB) "Remaking Our Heartlands" program. By making use of infill sites and redevelopment opportunities to inject more good quality housing and upgrade the living environment in established towns, it is possible to create more homes in familiar places. These new developments help ensure that facilities keep up with changing needs. Moreover, providing nearby replacement housing for those affected by redevelopment enables communities to stay in place to the largest extent possible.

Another important consideration is conserving our built heritage amidst rapid development. Despite development pressures, close to seventy-two hundred buildings and structures have been conserved in more than one hundred conservation areas through a comprehensive conservation program. Many of these buildings are conserved within the context of the preservation of entire districts, and have been successfully put to adaptive reuse. These serve as important physical anchors to Singapore's sense of local character, history, and identity.

A "CITY IN A GARDEN"

Creating a good quality of life goes beyond providing buildings and appropriate facilities. Despite Singapore's land constraints, the provision of greenery is prioritized in tandem with urban development. An extensive network of parks, park connectors, and waterways has been safeguarded to provide green relief and recreational opportunities. In order to further integrate greenery into the city, sky-rise and vertical greenery are encouraged to make Singapore a "City in a Garden."

Despite being a small country, great efforts have been made in Singapore to protect its natural areas and biodiversity. Today, close to 10 percent of Singapore is set aside for green spaces, even as it continues to grow. Singapore accordingly has four nature reserves, twenty nature areas, and other green spaces such as parks and sky-rise greenery.

STRATEGIES FOR ENVIRONMENTAL SUSTAINABILITY

To ensure environmental sustainability, there is an emphasis on developing in an environmentally responsible manner by using resources efficiently and minimizing negative impacts on the environment. The quality of the living environment is further safeguarded through ensuring the compatibility of adjacent land uses and implementing the necessary safety, health, and pollution buffers.

Singapore has made consistent efforts to achieve a diversified, adequate, and sustainable supply of water through increasing local water catchment. Similar efforts have been made in developing effective waste management practices. Since Sin-

gapore does not have enough landfills, more than half of its waste is recycled, and almost all the rest is incinerated. Today, only 2 percent of the solid waste generated in Singapore ends up in its only landfill facility, the Pulau Semakau Landfill site, which was created between two offshore islands and began operating during the nineteen-nineties.[5] Moreover, as a result of efforts to maintain biodiversity and careful pollution-prevention measures, this landfill site coexists in a region rich in biodiversity.

Mobility and transportation are key to ensuring that high-density cities function efficiently. For Singapore, promoting public transport is a key strategy in meeting the population's mobility needs in a sustainable manner since public transport is more resource efficient and creates less air pollution than high levels of dependency on private cars. Plans are

General View of Singapore's Marina Bay.

being made to expand Singapore's rail transit network by 2030 so that eight in ten households are within a ten-minute walk from a train station. Timely investments in public transportation, expansion of the public transportation network, and the prioritization of road utilization for public transportation are essential steps in extending the reach and service standards for public transportation so that it increasingly provides a convenient alternative to the automobile.

Beyond this, environmentally friendly precincts that are "car-lite" as well as pedestrian and cyclist friendly are being planned and developed. We at URA are working with various agencies on a National Cycling Plan to build a safe and extensive network of over seven hundred kilometers of cycling paths island wide to facilitate cycling as a sustainable travel mode.

STRATEGIES TO OPTIMIZE LAND AND SPACE

To make the best use of Singapore's limited land and sea resources, different strategies to conserve and optimize the use of land are being consciously adopted. Efforts are made to cluster high-density residential and commercial developments around transport nodes, prioritize development in built-up areas, co-locate facilities to minimize land take, expand land capacity by optimizing the use of underground spaces for infrastructure and utilities, as well as incorporate land efficient infrastructure and technology where possible, as is the case with the Common Services Tunnel (CST).[6]

PRAGMATISM AMIDST COMPETING NEEDS

Like other cities, as Singapore continues to grow, it will invariably face difficult choices as increasing urbanization will necessitate intensive changes in the physical landscape. Maintaining a long-term, holistic, and pragmatic approach towards land use planning will enable Singapore to look at the issues objectively, balance different needs, and make the necessary trade-offs for the greater good. We strive to adopt an integrated planning process that makes it possible to take a long-term view of growth opportunities and challenges, plan in advance to balance competing land requirements, and make carefully considered trade-offs. Carrying out these planning strategies requires extensive coordination between various government agencies, and is a "Whole of Government" effort. Singapore is unique in the sense that it has a single level of government, which aids in the coordination process. Nonetheless, there is a need for an institutionalized process that brings together the different government agencies involved in economic, social, environmental, and infrastructural development.

To be able to build consensus and garner support for the choices being made, it is also necessary to engage the public. In addition, it is an important step in building rooted and cohesive communities, and helps in refining plans and ensuring that planning efforts meet the people's needs. The public is consulted and its feedback is sought through different platforms. Educational programs, idea competitions, online consultations, as well as industry and community dialogues are avenues used to reach out to the community.

CONCLUSION

Globalization and urbanization will continue to pose challenges to cities in Asia, particularly in relation to issues such as overcrowding and environmental sustainability. Not all growth is bad, however. With appropriate plans and policies, targeted and inclusive growth can improve the well being of urban populations. We as planners need to look at the challenges of urban growth holistically, and to take a pragmatic approach in balancing different needs and trade-offs while seeking the support of those affected by the choices we make.

1 For information regarding Singapore's natural reserves and areas, see https://www.nparks. gov.sg/biodiversity/our-ecosystems/nature-ar-eas-and-nature-reserves.

2 The Quality of Living Index survey by Mercer Human Resource Consulting rated Singapore the best place to live in Asia, see http://www.uk.mer-cer.com/newsroom/2015-quality-of-living-sur-vey.html.

3 For additional information on the URA's Master Plan 2014, see https://www.ura.gov.sg/uol/mas-ter-plan/View-Master-Plan/master-plan-2014/master-plan/Key-focuses/economy/Economy.

4 For additional information on Marina South, see https://www.ura.gov.sg/uol/master-plan/view-master-plan/master-plan-2014/master-plan/Regional-highlights/central-area/central-area/Marina-south.aspx.

5 Regarding the Semakau Landfill, see http://www.nea.gov.sg/docs/default-source/ener-gy-waste/waste-management/sl_tmts-2015-brochure.pdf.

6 The CST is a network of underground tunnels housing utility networks serving the Marina Bay area. It maximizes the use of underground space and optimizes land use by freeing up road rights of way typically set aside for utilities.

Constructing Urban Landscapes: New Infrastructures

BRUNO DE MEULDER and KELLY SHANNON

Infrastructure has always canalized the flows of urbanization. In addition to being move-ment conduits, transportation networks are connectors and collectors, sources of com-munication and exchange for people and programs, and as such they also are places that define the quality of the urban realm. This quality has everything to do with the intensity of exchanges, communications, and movements. The logical conjunction of transporta-tion and development stems from the fact that with the imposition of infrastructure on a territory, the landscape becomes open to domestication. Evidently, infrastructure is part and parcel of regional and urban structuring. Throughout the two-sided history of urbanism, infrastructure has been explicitly designed to initiate, guide, and structure set-tlement patterns. Besides physical structuring (which is one of its sides) urbanism also stands for—as Louis Wirth put it—a way of life (the other side).[1] Since time immemorial, infrastructure has been viewed as a generator of urbanity, and a means by which to struc-ture forms and modes of public life. Infrastructure by definition is public space, the space that makes the built environment transcend the purely functional or economic.

Linking the productive countryside to settlements, canals, roads, and, later, rails, all have formed linear systems of urbanism that tied movement, commerce, exchange, habitation, and so many other forms of urban life into vibrant filaments, which, in turn, have served as initiators of larger development networks: grids, suburban allotments, and eventually highways and ring roads. There is a rich legacy of historical examples of transportation infrastructure that link forms of transportation to urban morphology. The world's built landscapes, engendered by accessibility, have become part of market mechanisms. They spring from processes of urbanization in which the overall built form of the territory is shaped by successive incremental and sometimes radical interventions that respond to the land or real estate value of their location, and to the indirect return on investment of transportation infrastructure development. In many contexts, the configurative and structuring capacity of infrastructure networks across various scales—from the territory to the city—and the manner in which they underline different places afford surplus values to infrastructure beyond utilities related to mobility and communication, as well as the supply of goods, water, gas and the like.[2]

The rich bequest of built works of urbanism proves that properly planned and designed infrastructure can qualitatively guide urbanization in a manner that does not merely sur-render to the volatile movement of investment capital and power through the creation of logical, systemic, and interdependent relationships. In Paris, Georges-Eugène (Baron) Haussmann modernized the medieval capital between 1852 and 1870 with networks of boulevards that were both brutally imposed on the fabric and embedded in it, and that took advantage of existing monument, topography, and real estate opportunities. Sec-tional richness was precisely designed, and the landscape, street furniture, building edg-es, and utilities below the surface were all built concurrently, and formed the city's sys-tem of transportation (including public transportation), promenades, utilities, and power. Simultaneously, they make a new urban environment with an omnipresence of trees and other natural elements. The systematic reintroduction of nature through interconnected systematic tree lines along boulevards and parks such as the Bois de Boulogne and the

Bois de Vincennes were instruments of urban naturalization, an operation that is considered necessary to humanize the artificial and hectic urban world, and to turn the urban into a natural habitat for mankind. Haussmann consequently combined water and fire: a modern integrated infrastructure system of roads, sewage lines, gas pipes, and the like that simultaneously incorporated the archetype of the human habitat: a natural environment full of trees that invited all types of social practices. The functional and the natural overlapped and coexisted.

Similarly, in the United States, Frederick Law Olmsted's Boston Back Bay Fens and Emerald Necklace (1878–96) cleverly integrated landscape, infrastructure, and architecture to achieve not only a horizontal (planar) juxtaposition of various uses (including vehicular, recreational, and representational spaces) and linkages across various scales (with distinctive places in the city and as part of a larger territorial system), but also sections that included underground infrastructural improvements (subways, sewage lines, water mains, et cetera). The Emerald Necklace, which consists of a 1,100-acre chain of nine parks linked by parkways and waterways, is simultaneously a tidal mitigation system, an automobile parkway, a real estate development project, a public park, and a site for urban gardens, all related to an even larger metropolitan system of parks and parkways. In New York, Robert Moses propelled—during America's post-Depression era onwards—the notion of the parkway as a system of choreographed high-speed vehicular routes through ribbon-like parks. Park systems accordingly became integrated into the reasoning of urban infrastructure development. Moses's parkways were inscribed in the metropolitan conception of a city that melded landscape, infrastructure, and urbanization. Infrastructure in the examples of Haussmann, Olmsted, and Moses transcended the purely functional. Infrastructure was not yet reduced to the pure sectoral product that it eventually evolved into during the era of the highway, where it became the sole responsibility of departments of transportation and public works.

The infrastructure of the twenty-first century must surely build upon the legacy of Haussmann, Olmsted, Moses, and others who conceived of integrative systems in which the organization of urbanism and network systems worked with the development of the collective realm. The infrastructure of today clearly must address the formative power of the network, but also that of larger environments and our world's contemporary challenges, namely climate change and fast globalization, particularly in the non-Western world. Therefore, the elaboration of distinctive design solutions that stress the *genius loci* of the localities that the network serves is more necessary than ever. Ecological infrastructure can be designed and can work as a component of resilience in the face of what Canadian ecologist C. S. Holling describes as an evolutionary perspective in the search for safe-fail designs that encompasses the notion of a *dynamic* state of equilibrium at the scale of systems.[3] The conventional worldview on the domestication of landscapes as a representation of appropriation by man is increasingly reversed according to a perspective where man is simply another layer situated upon a far vaster ecological system. Ecological reserves allow, in the long run, for the definition of green and blue frames in which further urban development may be embedded. The redefinition of infrastructure—from roads to nature—is exactly what a new phase of landscape urbanism projects seek to accomplish. The following two projects by our design and research institute Research Urbanism and Architecture (RUA) demonstrate this approach of landscape urbanism.

URBAN FORESTRY, SPACE FOR WATER, AND "SMART DENSIFICATION": HOOG KORTRIJK, BELGIUM, 2012

In Belgium, the city of Kortrijk (population 75,000) is the capital of a region known as the "Texas of Flanders," a fragmented and diffused territory characterized by a simultaneity of differences, which is a gentle way to characterize its chaotic morphology where industry and housing are scattered everywhere over the territory (FIG. 1). It is a region that is still growing, with its small and medium-size industries, colleges, urban services, and residential developments that consume the already little remaining landscape. The center of the city is situated on the Leie River, forty-two kilometers from Ghent and twenty-five kilometers from Lille, and is part of the Eurométropole (Lille-Kortrijk-Tournai), which houses 1.9 million inhabitants. Founded in the Middle Ages, the city, which originally accumulated its wealth from flax and wool, is now known as an entrepreneurial center with a diverse economy extending from energy and defense industries to services. The flexibility inherent in this diverse network of predominantly small and medium-size often linked enterprises is frequently thought to be a form of resilience as it allows fast adaptation to changing market conditions. Until today, Europe's economic crisis has not hit Belgium as hard as it hit some of the continent's southern nations, but the impact is nonetheless evident. Public authorities are, for example, no longer able to follow the increase in traffic with infrastructure extensions that could canalize the ever-growing flow of cars.

In 2012, a plan was developed for Leiedal, an intermunicipal organization in Southwest Flanders, to rethink Hoog Kortrijk, the car-based, postwar extension of Kortrijk located

FIG. 1: The "Texas of Flanders."
Kortrijk is a densely occupied, but diffuse urban territory in Southwest Flanders.
The egg-shaped highway node generates the centrality of Hoog Kortrijk, the nondescript space
where a number of large built structures of regional importance stand in splendid isolation.

south of the medieval historic core, and the E17 highway that was built along functionalist
lines of separation. Dispersed urban functions had been relocated here, which gave way
to an archipelago of large monofunctional elements. These elements are often comprised
of grouped and previously separated schools, hospitals, et cetera. The overall area today
needs densification, a new vitality, and, above all, spatial cohesion. Large-scale big-box

buildings mark the territory, and visitors to its Xpo center, regional hospital, health facilities, business parks, retail stores, regional colleges, and university come by private car and do not linger in the area. With the exception of a few fragmented residential enclaves, the area does not house the usual range of daily urban activities (disregarding perhaps the gas station that also happens to include a newspaper shop).

Further fragmentation of the dense, yet diffuse territory remains the greatest threat to the remaining open landscape, and remains one of the main obstacles to a more sustainable development. Excessive building and fragmentation has led to erosion problems. Exces-

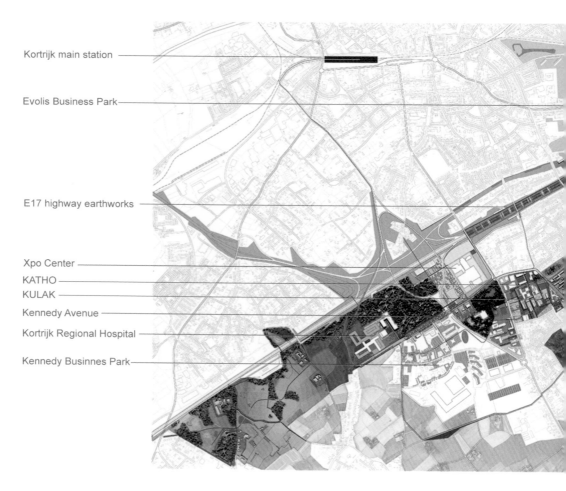

FIG. 2: Green-Blue Framework.
The Hoog Kortrijk master plan anchors the area in a regional green structure while providing a robust green-blue framework that accommodates future development. This creates a new public realm that recontextualizes and gives a shared, common platform to the area's existing fragmented services and isolated programs.

sive covering by asphalt, construction, and other impermeable groundcover has caused more flooding downstream and has increased erosion. The predicted consequences of climate change will worsen these effects. The suburban atmosphere of Hoog Kortrijk is continually changing due to regional interventions along the E17 highway. These include the recent construction of the aforementioned large hospital by Swiss architects Baum-schlager Eberle, which is slated for continual expansion, the 55,000 square meter Xpo center, colleges such as KATHO, the Kennedy and Evolis Business Parks, as well as the enlargement of the "knowledge axis" of the regional branch of the University of Leuven

(KULAK). Amidst such monofunctional and monolithic elements, enclaves of middle-class housing organize their own introverted environments that are so typical of the "diffused city" of Flanders.[4] The original countryside composition of farms and rolling hills remains only visible at the southern extents of Hoog Kortrijk. A finely meshed patchwork of farms is nestled with remarkable regularity in the topographic and hydrologic structure of the territory. This is in contrast to the rest of the landscape, which has been overwhelmed by the indiscriminate juxtaposition of urban, industrial, and rural fabrics.[5]

Our proposed project utilized infrastructure and landscape to reorient and requalify Hoog Kortrijk. A number of earthworks along the noisy E17 highway define a baseline for the project. They create a sound barrier for the adjacent environment while organizing the transition of the city's service area to the open countryside, and, more importantly, host in their section profiles new infrastructure services such as a regional public transportation system. The bundling of infrastructure avoids increased land consumption and creates synergies. The old infrastructure axis of Hoog Kortrijk, which was named Kennedy Avenue in the nineteen-sixties, is a dysfunctional express road, since it is located much too close to the E17 highway exit to be able to take up its intended role as a flowing traffic distributor. The plan proposes that this road be relieved of cars and turned into a "soft" spine that is dedicated to public transportation, bicycles, and pedestrians. It is to be anchored within a series of earthworks that connect the major service destinations. It also functions as a collector for the mostly perpendicular and soft mobility lines between the urban and the countryside—each of which has a different character, connecting main urban civic elements, schools, parks, and industrial zones (FIG. 2).

FIG. 3: Vegetal Infrastructure.
A rich variety of existing and new forest typologies with a broad palette of tree types
and plant species create a wide eco-tone, allowing for diverse atmospheres and generating
new ecologies and recreational settings for Hoog Kortrijk.

In addition, an ambitious public transportation system was envisioned to connect regional facilities to the wider territory. Rapid trams would link not only the city center of Kortrijk to Hoog Kortrijk, but also develop a transportation network for the fragmented territory of the highly urbanized southwest of Flanders. The network includes nodes that focus on new areas of centrality (such as the regional hospital) that will become public transportation hubs. The modal shift from car-oriented to public transportation would be enhanced by the development of a civic spine, which would in turn generate a significant and substantial, but completely new type of public space, and would help generate a new form of public life that is based on urbanism. Moreover, car parking areas would be (re)designed as park-like areas that accommodate a decreasing number of vehicles. They also would be an integral component of a comprehensive storm water management system and an extensive tree-planted green network. This will solve flooding problems downstream and temper erosion, while inducing environmental quality.

A green and blue framework in which the downsized road infrastructure would be embedded is defined and forms the canvas of the project. It is simultaneously intended as part of a larger territorial system that has the capacity to forcefully guide urban densification (through the sheer mass of trees), create a new identity for the area, build upon the existing water bodies and pockets of forest structures, increase biodiversity, and extend landscape mosaics. Within this unifying framework, a rich variety of existing and new forest typologies with a broad palette of plant species are proposed to create a wide eco-tone, allowing for diverse atmospheres and generating new ecologies and recreational settings (FIG. 3). Space for water, in addition to vegetated swales and roadside channels, would include a large retention basin. The basin is part of the existing creek and lowland system that lies between the housing, the university, and the Evolis Business Park area. There is also a water square on the urban platform near the hospital, as well as a series of shallow cascades and water gardens to animate the pubic space along the civic spine. "Smart" densification of the university, college, and student housing would occur along the new public infrastructure system and afforested areas (FIG. 4). Although urban development in the past was steered through the development of road infrastructure, further development would now be guided by the structure of the evolving landscape, which is defined by afforested areas, water, and other green structures such as wetlands, marshes, orchards, et cetera. This will define a robust frame in which further densification is possible without new road building. On the contrary, roads and parking lots may be downsized, thereby finally giving space to pedestrians, or may simply be completely converted into carless public spaces. Accordingly, the above-mentioned Kennedy Avenue would become a civic spine.

Extension of the university is embedded within forest pockets and the topography is used to integrate limited parking.

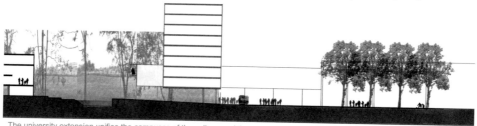

The university extension unifies the campuses of the college and the university, creates synergies between the two, and with a new tramway station, creates a point of gravity and intensity within the natural quietness of the landscape.

The section of Kennedy Avenue in front of the new regional hospital is reconfigured into a visitors' parking area that marks the edge of a large-scale, serene square that recontextualizes the hospital.

FIG. 4: "Smart" Densification.
"Smart" densification of the university, college, and student housing blocks generates synergies and allows for the integration of a public transportation hub. The densification would occur along the new public infrastructure network and afforested areas. In contrast to past practices, when road infrastructure steered urban development, future development will now be canalized by the landscape structure, which is defined by afforested areas, water, and tree-lined boulevards. The landscape structure defines a simultaneously open and robust frame in which densification is possible without new road building.

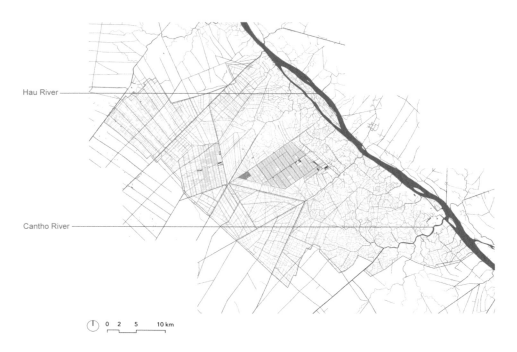

0   2   5   10 km

FIG. 5: Water as Register.
The main identity of the Vietnamese city of Cantho (founded at the confluence of the Hau and
Cantho Rivers) is connected to its relationship to the Hau River, with its perpendicular
tributaries, numerous navigable and irrigation canals, and the river system's natural islands.
The manmade canal landscape of Indochina was inscribed into the natural waterscape
of the rivers between the eighteenth and twentieth centuries. The water network is the vein system
of the territory, which, depending on the season, drains water from, or supplies water to
each plot according to the rhythm of the seasons and prevailing tides.

DOUBLING A POPULATION: CANTHO, VIETNAM, 2010–2013

Cantho (population 1.2 million) in Vietnam faces completely different challenges than
Hoog Kortrijk. A landscape urbanism approach, however, seems appropriate here also
to engage with contemporary development conditions. Cantho is located in the heart
of the enormous floodplain of the Mekong delta, at the confluence of the Hau (lower branch of the Mekong) and Cantho Rivers (FIG. 5). The French colonial enterprise in
Indochina (1876–1954) radically transformed the Mekong delta's liquid landscape, which consisted of plains of reeds, marshes, and mangroves, into a highly productive, irrigated territory
in which almost all land is domesticated. The Mekong delta, which consists of an incredible
patchwork of nearly flat, irrigated lowlands, is known as Vietnam's "rice basket." Cantho is the
delta's most important and rapidly urbanizing city (primarily due to urban-rural migration). As

is the case throughout the country, the predicted effects of climate change—sea level rise and its effects (flooding, salination, and erosion) to begin with—are daunting. Moreover, its ongoing hectic modernization process includes the development of road-based urbanism, which consumes extremely rich agricultural land with ever-increasing speed, scale, and intensity. The long-term value of such construction is questionable. The extreme climate (hot and humid) and the soil's poor bearing capacity remain a real challenge for construction techniques. Still, the accessibility and connectivity afforded by the new roads, including the recently opened Hau River Bridge, have radically enhanced Cantho's strategic location. Urbanization is consequently growing exponentially.

FIG. 6: Organized Dispersal.
The development of Cantho envisions an alternative linearity. Instead of a continuous built-up strip along the river (as is the case in so many generic waterfront cities), it creates differentiated urban and rural centralities. The highway trajectory parallel to the Hau River is retraced to safeguard the dense mesh of orchards in Phong Dien. Similarly, the upstream landscape along the river is protected as a green complement for the new urban center of Omon, which is set back from the river and linked directly to the new highway. Instead of developing a homogeneous giant platform, the future Cantho assembles a set of centers, each with its own identity, and each orchestrating a different interplay with the Hau River, highway, civic spine, and linear park.

Cantho's expanding hybrid territories, though still primarily rural, face spatial limitations due to the intermingling of built-up environments and agricultural land, which increases conflicting claims on the territory. This is evident in the conflicts between urban and rural functions, as well as the ecological complexities caused by the presence of different water management methods, including natural and controlled floodplains, and wastewater treatment infrastructure. One of the main environmental threats affecting Cantho is the exponentially increasing loss of absorptive low lands, which are inadvertently filled with up to two meters of soil to provide protection from flooding and to support rather low-quality urbanization. Moreover, the absorptive capacity of the land is diminished as the amount of paved areas increase. The side effects of this include faster rainfall run-off and a lowering of the natural groundwater table. Problems relating to water quantity are mainly related to hydrological extremes that a daily tidal influence accentuates even further: high flow discharges and flood risks along rivers and urban drainage systems; and low flow discharges along rivers. The balance between hydraulic, ecological, agricultural, and urban (housing, industrial, and recreational) uses of space is ultimately far from optimal. In addition, as Cantho's urban core is continuously expanding, its drainage and sewage systems, which are often un-hygienically mixed, are becoming overstressed, and their integrity is jeopardized. This is only one of the sources of conflict that are increasingly dividing the city from its rural hinterland, even though Cantho's identity until now remains very much anchored in its profound embeddedness in and intense contact with the surrounding countryside.

The encroachment on water bodies alters ecologies and affects the severity and frequency of flooding, not to mention aggravating environmental degradation and pollution. In a revision of the city's master plan up to 2030, the RUA proposed soft engineering approaches in order to orient the development of Cantho towards resilience and adaptability, while accommodating its growth to a predicted two million inhabitants in a form of dispersed urbanization (FIG. 6). The plan, made between

FIG. 7: Cantho's Natural Forests.
The existing green structure is directly related to topography and to hydraulic management. The lowlands accordingly consist of paddy fields; and the intermediate and very fertile level of deposited sediments primarily consists of orchards.
The Phong Dien area to the city's southwest covers a tight network of Cantho River tributaries with banks of intermediate height that assemble one of the most extraordinary collections of orchards in the world.

2010 and 2012 by the RUA in cooperation with Vietnam's Southern Institute of Urban and Rural Planning (SIUP), was approved by the Vietnamese Prime Minister in August 2013. It sought to give a simultaneously stable and flexible framework to the city's hectic development, which is driven by the spontaneity of bottom-up market forces, and is also complemented by considerable public investments in infrastructures.[6]

A structural interweaving of hydrology, soil conditions, and a new urban morphology is combined with the creation of a manipulated topography that rearticulates the existing landscape logic of the territory. In other words, the design interprets the nature and characteristics of the landscape, and attempts to work with them as much as possible. The delta's agricultural territory is basically generated through the inscription of canal systems—precolonial and French—in the natural water structures. The master plan revision constructs Cantho's future urban structure on similar lines: interweaving a green-blue structure and an urban structure. The green network is composed of the orchards in the area of Phong Dien, which is located to the south of Cantho, and is reputed for its floating market (FIG. 7). The green network also includes the proposed regional-scale Hau River high-tech agricultural park, which is part of the master plan's aim at realizing technological innovation in agriculture and aquaculture. Both large-scale areas are located along the higher land of the riverbanks. The high-tech agricultural park is located along the Hau River; the Phong Dien area is located at the confluence of the Hau and Cantho rivers and the latter's multitude of winding tributaries. The Cantho Linear Park, which extends over fifty kilometers in length, hosts recreational functions, and is connected to the extensive tree-planting program of the "civic spine." These spaces, together with the urban areas, are located on the highest—and thus safest—level in terms of flooding (FIG. 8).

The differentiation in topographical levels and soil conditions will allow for the use of a wide variety of tree specimens that may roughly be seen as forming a trilogy. The first component of this trilogy would be the paddy fields at the lowest levels, which are seasonally flooded with water and alternate with existing patches of more natural marshes. The second component would consist mostly of linear elements that are located on natural or artificial embankments situated between the riverbanks, which in themselves are the result of sedimentation. The third component of the trilogy would be located at the highest level, and would function as the civic spine and as "urban platforms," that is, the safe area for human habitation. At the highest level, ornamental greenery would also fine-tune the microclimate while contributing to the stabilization of artificial land. These last and mostly linear plantations would reactivate and amplify the ancient Asian tradition of tree planting along roads. This approach of variation that is dependent upon height is a subtle one. Height differences between each of the components are limited to approximately one meter or so.

The linear elements located in between these different levels and the paddy fields are the two major elements of the green structure. These also will safeguard the agricultural identity of the city, and as such dissolve recent antagonisms between city and countryside. Instead of allowing the expanding city to distort and fragment the countryside, the green framework guarantees a coherence of the countryside. A variety of urban centers

Civic Spine south (urban area): in the southern part of O Mon, with a symmetrical configuration and public transportation in the center

Civic Spine south (open landscape): between O Mon and existing Cantho, with tree planting of majestic proportions

FIG. 8: Trees in the City.

A generous profile, as is the case throughout Vietnam for express roads, marks the width of the civic spine, which is composed of a complex assemblage and applies cut-and-fill principles.
The profile is systematically planted with trees and incorporates storm water management, parking, and a hierarchy of different types of circulation systems, including public transportation, cars, and motorbikes. Additional traffic lanes may be added as new capacity is needed over time.
In the meantime, the planted profile will mature into a majestic place. The profile, while keeping some elements strictly fixed throughout all segments of its trajectory, simultaneously adapts itself to the different contexts it passes through, whether the existing city, new urban or rural centers, agricultural land in-between, or parks. It thereby creates complementary sets of atmospheres and microclimates that are generated by the extensive tree planting along the spine. This allows for the development of different types of planned and unplanned as well as formal and informal public uses, and allows this profile to obtain a civic character over time.

Civic Spine north (urban area): in the northern part of O Mon, with assymetrical mobility lanes which are slightly elevated, allowing clear views of the landscape

Civic Spine north (open landscape): between Thot Nhot and O Mon, with orchards and a rhythm of openings to accentuate views to the Hau River and the expansive river park

of relatively limited size would be embedded in the countryside. Each of these elements of this polycentric city-in-the-making would be in close contact with the countryside and its green constituent elements.

The blue network is designed to address both water quantity (that is, flooding, storm water retention, drainage, and irrigation) and water quality, and would be realized by a rigorous enforcement of the cut and fill balance principle during the process of urbanization (FIG. 9). Whenever land is artificially filled, a same amount of land is cut to rebalance the water storage capacity. This green-blue structure would define the counter-figure for "urban platforms," which would be located on raised artificial land. It also will become the backbone of the city along which its different centers would be anchored, and it will inscribe itself to a large extent into the natural water structure and soil conditions. In other words, the structuring of the landscape, which in itself is not much more than an articulation and exploitation of the already existing natural structure, would be the foundation for a new regional and urban form. With this, the ordering of the polycentric city-in-the-making would get a completely new character and nature. It is no longer the road infrastructure that defines the structure and the image of the city, as historically has been the case in most other cities. The structure of the future city would be its blue-green net, a flexible, but straightforward frame that is dynamic and evolving, and that is informed by existing landscape conditions, while simultaneously accommodating and shaping urban tissues that rationalize and modernize the Mekong delta's building traditions. It explicitly addresses the predicted consequences of climate change and increased flooding (FIG. 10). The expand-

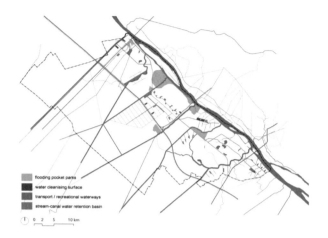

flooding pocket parks
water cleansing surface
transport / recreational waterways
stream-canal water retention basin

0   2   5   10 km

FIG. 9: Water Network.
The projected water network addresses both water quantity (flooding, storm water retention, drainage, and irrigation) and water quality (sewage and purification) issues. It marries them, where appropriate, to a more contemplative and recreational use of water. Elements in the water system consist of storm water channels and eco-swales that are coupled with the road network; "elastic parks," which work as sponges and thus can accommodate seasonal differences of water volume in the river; a decentralized wastewater purification network; a series of water retention basins consisting of lakes and ponds that are connected to a network of natural rivers; and man-made canals.

ing city and its peripheral territory are planned as a juxtaposition of characters and scale resulting from an orchestration of the infrastructural net, its natural green and blue systems, its topographical differences, its soil conditions, and also the programs allocated to these different levels and soils.[7]

DESIGNING RESILIENT CITIES: TOPOGRAPHIES OF CHANGE

In the Belgian project, the assignment was essentially to reedit the existing urban environment. As is the case in most Western contexts, the process of development is one of transformation, optimization, and correction, rather than of accommodating massive demographic, social, and economic growth in new urban areas. In this reediting, attempts were made to restate the balance between city and nature, between consumptive and productive space, between impermeable and porous surfaces, and between the urban and the rural. This rebalancing is realized by strategically shifting the design focus from urban structures such as Kortrijk's road systems to the landscape as a structuring framework to begin with, and, after that, as a receptor of activities. In short, the European project attempts to transform the territory primarily through the conscious and structural (re)construction of nature, and in this way (re)acquires the capacity to frame and structure the urban. Nature consequently regains recognition as a basic infrastructure of the urban. In opposition to approaches from the nineteenth and twentieth centuries, however, nature is not controlled. The project rather works with nature and its forces, which in turn control the urban, rather than the opposite. The rearticulation and reconstruction of nature delivers the frame for any further development. It remains open to a variety of developments, or to none at all, considering that uncertainty is a main characteristic of the times. As the frame is natural, it also evolves over time according to its own rhythm that is distinct when compared to that of the built structures of the city.

low land (floodable in monsoon)
Cantho Linear Park
high land orchards
medium land orchards
Hau River productive park

0   2   5   10 km

FIG. 10: Choreographed Flooding.
Fertile higher land along the Hau River, which is a result of sedimentation, is strategically embedded into the green framework as the Hau River Park. This new type of park is a high-tech agricultural park that aims at realizing technological innovation in agriculture and aquaculture, and is safeguarded from urbanization by the fact that it will become a major contributor to the area's economy. When flooding occurs, settlements and orchards are "safe" since they are located on higher land, and low paddy land temporarily accommodates the floodwater. The Hau River Park is a cornerstone of Cantho's green network that guides the choreography of flooding.

In contexts like Vietnam, where urbanization, industrialization, and migration are galloping ahead, the reconstruction of nature needs to simultaneously take place along with massive ongoing urban development. The strategies proposed require that the cities and their territories address topographies of change through a spatial lens, but ones in which economy and ecology, both urban and natural, are diametrically opposed. Robust and substantial green and blue systems structure the territory and create frames for the adaptation of the landscape. Resilience is built in by designing an overlap of natural and built ecologies. The megacity in the making is tamed before it reaches uncontrollable dimensions and eats the countryside away. On the contrary, the expanding city is broken up, scaled, and distributed over the territory by the force of the blue-green frame.

Both RUA projects are attempts that aim at further articulating the definition of landscape urbanism, a more or less academic discipline that emerged in the nineteen-nineties, at a time when it became clear that dealing with the challenges of contemporary cities, be it in brownfield conditions in the West or hectic urbanization scenarios in the South, require a cross-scalar approach that stretches from the scale of the territory to that of the road, and that simultaneously combines the abstract and conceptual and the tangible and concrete in order to comprehend thinking in the form of plans as well as in terms of process. It is based on merging landscape architecture and urbanism. Landscape architecture provides an age-old capacity to articulate and scale the territory and the concrete details of vegetation and its inherent process-oriented approaches. Urbanism allows for structural approaches, and is characterized by a quest for rationality. Their merging into landscape urbanism indeed is a logical theoretical proposition. The projects of the RUA validate the underlying hypotheses of landscape urbanism through actual projects. These are commissioned by concrete agencies searching for more appropriate forms of planning that are able to deal with the challenges of our time. These RUA projects, which were developed in cooperation with the commissioners of Leiedal in Belgium and SIUP on behalf of the Cantho People's Committee, inscribe themselves in the landscape and in a geographic-morphological logic that is detected through a careful analysis and sensitive observation of collaborating multidisciplinary teams. Such inherent logic of the landscape allows for a mastering of the large scale with relative simple means: applying the tool of the section and profile. Such minimal interventions result in maximum effects. In that sense they are topographical projects, and may be referred to as "Braille urbanism."

NOTES:

The Leiedel project was developed in a Landscape Urbanism workshop that was commissioned by Stadsbestuur Kortrijk in January 2012 for Hoog Kortrijk. It was run by B. De Meulder and K. Shannon with V. Cox, B. de Carli, S. Hoornaert, G. Lannoo, I. Llach, K. Lokman, M. Luegening, M. Motti, T. Ono, J. Provoost, P. Russo, C. Van der Zwet, and E. Vanmarke. Further development was carried out by B. De Meulder, K. Shannon, M. Motti, and I. Llach with S. Hoornaert and a team from Leiedal.

The Cantho master plan revision team included a Belgian team and a Vietnamese team. The Belgian team consisted of RUA, WIT Architecten, LATITUDE (K. Shannon, B. De Meulder, G. Geenen, C. Vilquin, P. Dudek, D. Derden, A. De Nijs, and R. Van Durme). The Vietnamese team consisted of N. Q. Hùng, L. P. Hin, T. N. Bınh (leaders), T. T. N. Sng, N. L. T. P. Tho, D. T. Quang (planning), T. N. Bınh (transport and land form), D. T. Thanh Mai (water supply), T. Q. Ninh (wastewater and sanitation), P. Q. Khánh (electric supply), N. V. Thng (planning management), and K. S. P. H. Tho (infrastructure management). The client was the Cantho People's Committee / Cantho Department of Construction.

1 Louis Wirth, "Urbanism as a Way of Life," *The American Journal of Sociology* 44, no. 1 (1938).

2 See, Kelly Shannon and Marcel Smets, *Landscape of Contemporary Infrastructure* (Rotterdam, 2010).

3 C. S. Holling, "Resilience and Stability of Ecological Systems," *Annual Review of Ecology and Systematics*, no. 4 (1973).

4 See, Bruno De Meulder, Jan Schreurs, Annabel Cock, and Bruno Notteboom, "Patching up the Belgian Urban Landscape," *OASE* 52 (1999).

5 See, Bruno De Meulder and Tania Vandenbroucke, "The Lys-Scheldt Interfluvium: Theater of Do-It-Yourself," *OASE* 63 (2004).

6 See, Kelly Shannon and Bruno De Meulder, "Revising the Cantho Masterplan, Vietnam: Pilotage of a Civic Spine in a Blue-Green Landscape Mesh," in *Water Urbanisms 2: East*, UFO3: Explorations in Urbanism, eds. Kelly Shannon and Bruno De Meulder (Zurich, 2013), pp. 138–161.

7 Ibid, pp. 154–55.

Afterword

MOHSEN MOSTAFAVI

How should we consider the design of our cities in the years to come? Are current planning tools and techniques capable of dealing with the challenges facing the built environment? What can we learn from the diversity of responses from across the globe to the conundrum of urbanization? And in what specific ways does planning in Asia require a different approach than in other parts of the world?

These were only some of the questions posed during the "Emerging Models of Planning Practices" seminar held in Singapore in 2012, which brought together a diverse group of participants from across the region. The intention of the discussion was to reflect on the current status of planning, with a specific emphasis on the lessons to be learned from Singapore.

The particular condition of Singapore—its climate, its economic, cultural, and political structure—has led to the articulation of a form of planning development that in many ways is unique in terms of its modes of practice. Here, the role of the Urban Redevelopment Authority (URA) has been instrumental in defining the relationship of this city-state to land development at multiple levels. The structure and authority of this government agency has far-reaching consequences with regard to issues such as responsibility, control, ownership, scalar interrelationships between planning and urban design, and the definition of public-private partnerships. Unlike many such organizations, the URA is not simply a policy making body; rather, it directly helps shape the form of the city—controls its skyline—through its design prototypes for specific sites. Compared to other contexts, the process for such things as permits is potentially more clear-cut.

The example of Singapore is interesting because it raises the question of the degree to which public agencies under the direction of the state should exercise control over the form of the city—a question that has particular relevance at a time when we are witnessing many planning agencies relinquishing their responsibilities with regard to urban development. In such a climate, Singapore provides a valuable case study and a stimulus to a vital discussion of the framework and limits of planning overall.

In many respects it is important to remind ourselves that the very tools of modernist planning have been legitimately questioned. The emphasis on the singular role of the master plan, as a predetermined vision to be executed in phases, clearly does not respond to the diversity of needs and geographic conditions that exist in different parts of the world. Yet it is not totally clear what the alternative strategies are.

This collection of essays is intended to address some of the ways in which we might conceive a new set of planning practices that are better able to address the needs of both citizens and the environment. Correspondingly, the dialogue between sustainable and social development forms the core of much of the writing. At the same time, in addition to these topics, it is critical to consider a multiplicity of other issues, from tangible and intangible heritage, to the enormous increase in population, to variations in climate, to the availability of resources, and to infrastructure—all of them necessary preconditions for a new, deliberate approach to planning.

Such an approach requires us to be cognizant of the particularities of a specific geography and sensitive towards the needs of the citizens. The aim should always be for planning to help improve the quality of life. But this type of intentional approach also requires new forms of knowledge and creativity that are able to do justice to the consideration of the many factors that help shape a particular situation.

We are at the beginning of a much-needed conversation about how we might bring together circumstance, intention, and proposition in the making of new urban conditions. The collection of essays in this book use examples from a variety of locations and practices to move towards this agenda. As much as in the essays themselves, however, it is in the gaps between the texts that we must find new clues on how to rethink planning in ways that make it more responsive to the need and the desire for a more democratic, productive, and pleasurable setting for human action.

MOHAMMAD AL-ASAD

Founding Director, Center for the Study
of the Built Environment, Amman
Member, 2013 and 2016 Aga Khan
Award for Architecture Steering
Committees

BRUNO DE MEULDER

Professor, Department of Architecture,
Katholieke Universiteit Leuven (KU
Leuven), Leuven
Cofounder, Research Urbanism and
Architecture (RUA), Leuven

FARROKH DERAKHSHANI

Director, Aga Khan Award for
Architecture, Geneva

ALEJANDRO ECHEVERRI

Director, URBAM, Center for Urban
and Environmental Studies, EAFIT
University, Medellín

WEIWEN HUANG

Director, Shenzhen Center for Design,
Shenzhen

LIM ENG HWEE

Chief Planner and Deputy
Chief Executive Officer, Urban
Redevelopment Authority, Singapore

CHRISTOPHER C. M. LEE

Cofounder and Principal, Serie
Architects, London

RAHUL MEHROTRA

Architect and Professor, Department
of Urban Planning and Design, Harvard
University Graduate School of Design,
Cambridge, MA
Member, 2013 Aga Khan Award for
Architecture Steering Committee

MOHSEN MOSTAFAVI

Dean and Alexander and Victoria Wiley
Professor of Design, Harvard University
Graduate School of Design, Cambridge,
MA
Member, 2013 Aga Khan Award for
Architecture Steering Committee;
2016 Aga Khan Award for Architecture
Master Jury

DENNIS PIEPRZ

Principal, Sasaki Associates, Boston

KAIS SAMARRAI

Executive Director, Lead Development,
Abu Dhabi
Visiting Professor, Urban Studies, New
York University–Abu Dhabi

KELLY SHANNON

Director, Master of Landscape
Architecture Program, The University of
Southern California, Los Angeles
Cofounder, Research Urbanism and
Architecture (RUA), Leuven

AARON TAN

Director, RAD Architects, Hong Kong

Power, Rights, and Emerging Forces:
New Models of Urban Planning Practice in China
Figs. 1 & 2: Weiwen Huang and
Urbanus Architects
Figs. 3 & 4: Weiwen Huang

Medellín Redraws its Neighborhoods:
Social Urbanism, 2004–11
Figs. 1, 3, 6, 7 & 8: Luigi Baquero
Fig. 4: Explora Park
Fig. 5: Municipality of Medellín

Seeding: An Architecture of the City
Figs. 1–10: Serie Architects

The City Campus: Models of Planning Processes
Figs. 1 & 7–10: Sasaki Associates
Figs. 2, 3, 5 & 6: Sasaki Associates / MKPL
Fig. 4: Dennis Pieprz

Future Heritage
Figs. 1, 2 & 6–11: RAD Architects
Fig. 3: Ian Lambot
Fig. 4: Aaron Tan
Fig. 5: Reproduced from Wikipedia (http://commons.
wikimedia.org/wiki/File:ShanghaiMissingFloors.jpg)

The Evolution of Abu Dhabi City's Urbanization
and the Sustainability Challenge
Figs. 00 & 8: Kais Samarrai
Fig. 1: Wikimedia Commons: https://commons.wiki-
media.org/wiki/File:United_arab_emirates_rel95.jpg
Figs. 2, 6 & 7: National Archives, Abu Dhabi
Figs. 3, 4, 5, 9, 10, 11 & 12: Abu Dhabi
Urban Planning Council
Fig. 13: Masdar City

Planning for Sustainable Growth in Singapore
Opening image: Allie Caulfield (www.flickr.com)
Fig. 00: Urban Redevelopment Authority, Singapore

Constructing Urban Landscapes:
New Infrastructures
Fig. 1: OSA: Research Group Urbanism
and Architecture, KU Leuven
Figs. 2–10: RUA

Every effort has been made to identify and
contact the copyright holders for the images
reproduced in this monograph. The publishers
will be happy to correct in subsequent editions
any errors or omissions that are brought to
their attention.

All websites cited in this publication were last
accessed in July 2016.

Editors

MOHAMMAD AL-ASAD
and
RAHUL MEHROTRA

Copyediting

LEINA GONZALEZ
CYRUS SAMII
IRENE SCHAUDIES

Graphic design

HANNES AECHTER

Typeface

SABON
NEUE HAAS

Production

FRANZISKA LANG
Hatje Cantz

Project management

ANNA IRENE SIEBOLD
Hatje Cantz

Reproductions

REPROMAYER GMBH
Reutlingen

Printing and binding

DZA DRUCKEREI
ZU ALTENBURG GMBH
Altenburg

Paper

150 g/m² LUXOART SAMT

2016 © Aga Khan Award for Architecture,
Hatje Cantz and authors

Published by
Hatje Cantz Verlag GmbH
Mommsenstraße 27
10629 Berlin
Germany
Tel. +49 30 3464678-00
Fax +49 30 3464678-29
www.hatjecantz.com
A Ganske Publishing Group company
Hatje Cantz books are available internationally
at selected bookstores. For more information
about our distribution partners, please visit our
website at www.hatjecantz.com.

ISBN 978-3-7757-4236-8

PRINTED IN GERMANY

Cover illustration:
Detail of Abdul Rahman Makhlouf's
"Guilding Concept Plan" for Abu Dhabi, 1968